FINDING COMMUNION

by

J. H. Churchill

formerly Dean of Carlisle

CHURCHMAN PUBLISHING LIMITED
1987

For
Elizabeth and David,
Tom, Oliver, and Freddie

FINDING COMMUNION
by
J. H. Churchill
was first published in Great Britain in 1987
by
CHURCHMAN PUBLISHING LIMITED
117 Broomfield Avenue
Worthing
West Sussex
BN14 7SF

Publisher: E. Peter Smith

and distributed to the book trade
by
BAILEY BOOK DISTRIBUTION LIMITED
Warner House
Wear Bay Road
Folkestone
Kent CT19 6PH

ISBN 1 85093 078 3

Printed and bound in Great Britain by
Biddles Limited, Guildford and King's Lynn

CONTENTS

FINDING COMMUNION

Introduction

Droppers into church on a Sunday, after a break of some years, are sometimes surprised to find that they drop into a communion service. 'It wasn't the ordinary service' they say, looking back to their childhood of many decades ago. A gentle response will assure them that communion has been the normal Christian Sunday service across the centuries, though there have been aberrations in this country from the beginning of the 18th century to the middle of our own. If the service was well done it may set those droppers-in looking for more, as it certainly does those who find their way in almost for the first time, perhaps as young parents. They may start from scratch with wondering just why Christians do this on Sunday mornings, and at the same time find an attraction in the movement of the communion service. There is certainly a need to provide help for those who start from scratch, to find their way not only to faith but to the focus of faith, the central act of communion. Such an exercise may be useful, too, to those who return to church after a gap of some years.

There are many who worship more or less regularly over the years who only gradually find their way to the centre of worship. It may be by moving from one area to another and discovering people who have found a much greater stimulus and fellowship around the altar than they had felt previously simply in the pew. Help is needed too for many other churchgoers to find communion at the centre. Such Christians reflect whole congregations, and their clergy too. They may just be aware that their worship needs renewing, or that their church has a number of separate congregations for separate services who never meet. They need to be helped to catch up with what has been one of the great movements of Christianity in the middle of the twentieth century – the Liturgical Movement. They need to appreciate the fact that among the many stirrings that shook the church in the 1960's, often in a direction of secularism, remarkably the one that had most effect was the revision of worship. This revision brought not only the opportunity to worship in direct language, but also to see the structures of what we are doing in the eucharist. These reforms ask for some simple account of how the church has found its way to a fresh perception of communion over the past decades.

Beyond this waits the renewal of the whole church in unity for mission. Though many of our discussions of ways to unity have centred on approaches to recognition of ministry, in the end the great need of the church is to put word and sacrament together and to put the common worship of the different parts of the church together. It has been significant that increasingly ecumenical bodies have come to see that the eucharist lies at the centre of Christian life and should itself unite word and sacrament, and that it itself relates us to the central work of Christ. So eucharist is the middle term of the great study of the Faith and Order Commission of the World Council, *Baptism, Eucharist, and Ministry*, which was sent out to the churches from the Lima conference in 1982. The section on the eucharist explains the considerable body of agreement reached by the theologians of the different churches, but also has some new and stimulating practical points to make. It says in one section, 'the Eucharist involves the believer in the central event of the world's history,' and later 'as the Eucharist celebrates the resurrection of Christ it is appropriate that this should take place at least every Sunday ... every Christian should be encouraged to receive communion frequently.' (p. 14)

The task for the Church can be seen against the background of the colour supplement world which has replaced the Sunday worship for many. That world is an intensely materialistic world in which there are great differences between rich and poor, where material is put both to noble beneficient ends, and to cruel and sensuous ones in a process that leaves people bewildered and hungry in mind. It is to this world that Jesus presents himself for our sustaining, through the cruelty of the crucifixion as a result of Middle East politics, but through his trust now made available to us by the power of his Father, working through his effective Spirit. He has given to us in this real and actual world, the simple food of bread and wine, to rich and poor alike.

Those who grope for something to take hold of in life, and who come to look at the Christian faith for the first time, or come back to it after some years, are unconsciously asking for help to find communion. Many Christians and congregations, beginning to awaken and grow, want to find their way; so too, do the divided churches of Christendom. Theologians now offer us a lively understanding of our involvement in the central event of the world's history in this sacrament. From all these angles we find the need for help to find communion.

*   *   *

These chapters have grown in response for explanations in parish, university, and cathedral congregations, as people have found their way to a rhythm of Christian worship around the altar. It owes much to three people – the vicar who inspired the parish where I served my first curacy, before he went on the become a suffragan bishop, Bishop C. L. P. Bishop – the bishop who set me thinking about helping a whole diocese from a liturgical committee, being himself a great liturgical pioneer, Bishop Leslie Brown – and more recently, to one of many friends in the ecumenical faculty of New College Edinburgh, Dr. Jan Tellini, who is himself secretary of the Scottish Episcopal Church Liturgical Committee.

1

SEE WHAT YOU FIND

Where do we begin to find communion? The Christian churches all claim to find their roots in the Bible, so this might be the obvious place to look first; that is the beginning, but for the development you have to look in the life of the churches, which is enshrined in their own books. So for many the place to look is in a prayer book. Certainly we want to look both in Bibles and prayer books before long, but the easiest place to look for communion is obviously where it is going on, in the churches. In this country we shall not have to look too far, but it is worth remembering that people in some other lands may face either the difficulty of distance or of political restrictions.

In many parts of this country there is a considerable choice offered. Though in some country districts it will be just the Church of England, this in itself presents a variety; but fairly constant through the variety of programmes and of notices offered is at least one communion service in each church on Sunday. It may simply be called 'Communion', from the act of receiving, or particularly if the service has some sung music about it, it may be called the 'Eucharist' – the Thanksgiving, one of the oldest names of the service from the fact that when Jesus blessed the bread or wine, he did it by thanking God for it. There will probably be offers of celebrations on weekdays as well as Sundays. This will almost certainly be so in a Roman Catholic church where three or four Masses may be offered on a Sunday, and others on weekdays, using the short name, Mass, which again caught on in the early centuries, once this service was said in Latin rather than Greek, from the final word of

9

dismissal. Many Free Churches now come to offer communion weekly, perhaps varying between the morning and the evening, some may still be monthly, and some of the Presbyterian tradition still quarterly; here it may be simply called the 'Lord's Supper', or the 'Breaking of Bread' from New Testament phrases.

Going in past these notice boards into the church you will in most cases find your vision focused on a table. It may indeed be at the far east end, or it may be surrounded by woodwork for preaching and reading in a Free Church, but now in some Anglican and Roman churches you will find the altar brought forward and more to the centre. If it is so brought forward it is likely to be a simple altar, but still with candles upon it. In some older churches altars still stand against the east end, and may be surrounded by curtains with seasonal colours hanging in front. The service may be very simple and quietly said, particularly in the early morning. It may be splendidly sung either by a large congregation or by a special choir leading a congregation, with an obvious effort in the offering of worship. There may be a different atmosphere of reflection and fellowship in an evening celebration, and this can be particularly true on a weekday, but again this can also be true of a quiet brief act in the morning.

It may be the discovery that some Christians go to communion on a weekday, and some indeed on many weekdays, or simply that some make a point of going to it every Sunday, that causes friends to ask 'Why so much communion?' At that stage it would be an unsatisfying answer to such enquirers to tell them that this has been at the centre of the church's worship right from the beginning; it will be useful to help them to discover this later. They can be better helped to look for the answer in their own homes in their own practice, and the way they say to their friends 'You must come in for a meal', or 'you must stop for a meal now', or 'you will need a meal before you go on'. They say that to their friends not only because they see their friend's need of sustenance, but also from their own need to express relationship in contact with their friends. The meal is a greater meeting place, it is the great subject for the invitations. It is not surprising that the Lord couches his invitation in these terms. The Last Supper must have been the last of many suppers of Jesus and his disciples, but the first of many for his subsequent followers.

The words and actions of Jesus in the Last Supper were more than a continuing invitation into the future; they were relating the actual supper to what was to follow in the next three days – the breaking of his body on the cross, the shedding of his blood, his dying in trust, and his being raised from the tomb. Through those events his followers found themselves changed from failure to forgiveness, from fear to courage, from confusion to communication. They found indeed the human situation changed; they found the pledge he had given them in the breaking of bread was true, that it gave them a way of renewing their life in his dying and rising life. The experience of Christians down the centuries has confirmed this. As the theologians drawn from all the traditions, Orthodox, Catholic, Anglican, Lutheran, Reformed and others, said in the LIMA text, 'The Eucharist involves the believer in the central event of the world's history'.

The involvement works both ways. We find that when we are offered the life of Jesus, dying and rising in communion, he asks us to be involved in the renewing of the world. We must certainly look into this both ways; we must look into the New Testament and the source and pledge, we must look through Christian experience, but then look on to where the Lord is leading us. It must not surprise us that he has been leading us through renewal of our actual worship in these last few decades to some new vistas of Christian responsibility in the world.

2

LOOK IN THE NEW TESTAMENT

We might expect to be told to look first in the gospels for anything concerned with Christian origins; even those who have studied the New Testament seriously need to be reminded that the letters of Paul to the churches were all written before the gospels which we have. We have strong evidence that Paul and Peter both met their death in the first great persecution under Nero; that persecution acted as a stimulus to produce the first presentation of the preaching and teaching about Jesus by Mark, probably a year or two later, with Matthew and Luke expanding this with other sources in the succeeding twenty years, and John providing his reflection and corrections from further sources ten years after that.

The earliest account of the Last Supper comes in Paul's first letter to the Corinthians. This is a letter written in reply to a number of queries that had been put to him when he was in Asia Minor, by visitors from a congregation he had formed in Corinth, and it also comments on reports from them. Communion obviously plays a central part in Paul's thoughts; he not only comments on what he hears about their practice, but he argues from it to try to bring them together. He hears of their splitting into groups, and he is concerned for their unity – 'We who are many are one body, for we all partake of the one bread', he says at one point (1 Corinthians 10.17). This extends an earlier argument to keep them clear of idol worship, when he says, 'I speak as to sensible men; judge for yourselves what I say. The cup of blessing which we bless, is it not a participation in the blood of Christ? The bread which we break, is it not a participation in the body of Christ?' (1 Corinthians 10.15 & 16).

Paul comments on the report of 'division among you' and then goes on to correct their disorder for their selfish eating and drinking when they meet together for the Lord's Supper. He tries to get them to stop and think what they are doing by reminding them of the tradition of the Lord's Supper that he had delivered to them, in 1 Corinthians 11.23, 'For I received from the Lord what I also delivered to you, that the Lord Jesus on the night when he was betrayed took bread, and when he had given thabnks, he broke it, and said, "This is my body which is broken for you. Do this in remembrance of me".' In the same way also the cup, after supper, saying, 'This cup is the new covenant in my blood. Do this, as often as you drink it, in rememrance of me'. It is important to realise wha a Jew such as Jesus, or as Paul, meant when he used the word 'remembrance', – in Hebrew 'zeker', in the Greek which Paul wrote, 'anamnesis'. He was not just looking back to the past at something gone, but claiming the past to be effective in the present. As Professor Anthony Hanson* puts it, 'When the Jew made a memorial of what God had done for his people in the past, he entered into the experience of the past and in some sense relived it or made it contemporary'. This was why Paul thought it was so important for Christians to realise what they were doing in their participation in the body and blood of Christ. So he went on to say, 'For as often as you eat this bread and drink this cup, you proclaim the Lord's death until he comes' (1 Corinthians 11.26). That death to Paul was the effective saving death which changed the human situation.

Paul certainly takes it very seriously because he goes on, 'Let a man examine himself, and so eat of the bread and drink of the cup. For anyone who eats and drinks without discerning the body eats and drinks judgement upon himself. That is why many of you are weak and ill, and some have died' (1 Corinthians 11.28–30). Paul shows us in other of his writings that he had a very vivid sense of the judgement of God in his dealings with his followers, and not surprisingly he sees it here. We may feel that

---

* Anthony Hanson – 'Church, Sacraments and Ministry' – Oxford 1975 p. 60

Paul stands rather too close to the emerging life of the church to see things in calm perspective. He certainly shows us how vividly and realistically he sees the relationship of the communicant to Christ and to the living events of Christ's death and resurrection. He also shows us how closely he took to be the relationship that Christ draws his followers in together. In fact, it looks as though it is from this thought of Christians sharing in the one bread, through which Christ gives them his body, that he goes on to develop the thought of Christians as the body of Christ, in the following chapter 12.

Paul does not stand alone; he had reminded those mixed up Christians in Corinth of the tradition he had passed on to them of the Last Supper. It was obviously part of the common stock of the church. So in the first gospel of Mark, written probably in the mid-sixties, ten years after Corinthians, we have a similar but slightly different account in Mark 14. 22–24, 'And as they were eating, he took bread, and blessed and broke it, and gave it to them, and said, "Take; this is my body." And he took a cup, and when he had given thanks he gave it to them, and they all drank of it. And he said to them, "This is my blood of the covenant, which is poured out for many".' This carries the overtones of the reference to the picture of the suffering of the Lord in Isaiah 53. 12, 'He poured out his soul to death . . ., yet he bore the sin of many'. This is expanded further in Matthew 26. 28, 'this is my blood of the covenant which is poured out for many for the forgiveness of sins'; spelling out more clearly the relationship with Christ in his work of meeting the world's wrong in his suffering and death, and bringing forgiveness through his resurrection. Luke has the interesting variation of giving the words for the cup before words for the bread (Luke 22 17–19). Not surprisingly some later texts of Luke then give a second cup after the bread in an attempt to bring Luke into line with Matthew and Mark. We have already seen that in the first passage in 1 Corinthians 10.6, when Paul is reminding them of the significance of communion, he refers first to the cup of blessing and then to the breaking of bread; when he goes on to give his account of the tradition of the Last Supper he puts it the other way around. It may be that the order of the bread and cup varied in the early church; the variations shown in Luke and Paul are not concerned with academic or historical interests, but very much with practice.

Luke's concern to help Christians find their present relationship with the risen Christ in their practice is seen not only in the Acts of the Apostles, but in his gospel itself. It is shown perhaps most clearly in the meeting of those two disciples on the road to Emmaus on Easter afternoon, who do not recognise the risen Christ at first, but only when he made the plan to stay with them at the end of their journey, and takes the bread and blesses it, and their eyes are opened. Later they tell 'How he was known to them in the breaking of bread' (Luke 24. 28–35). They also remark on how their hearts burned within them, 'while he opened to us the scriptures'. So the risen Christ is known to them through the scriptures and the breaking of bread, the two ingredients of Christian worship from the beginning, reflected through the centuries in the ministry of the word and the ministry of the sacrament.

In the Acts themselves the theme for the expansion for the mission of the risen Christ, through his followers, is set by the outpouring of the Spirit at Pentecost, and the first preaching of Peter answered by the response in baptism of many. The result is summarised by Luke in Acts 2 42, 'And they devoted themselves to the apostles' teaching and fellowship, to the breaking of bread and the prayers,' and it continues, 'and day by day, attending the temple together and breaking bread in their homes, they partook of food with glad and generous hearts, praising God and having favour with all the people'. Here in this setting of the beginning of the Church Luke sees the breaking of bread as central to the life of the growing church. Later, in accounts of Paul's travels, we have an example of the corporate life of groups of Christians springing up across the empire. In Acts 20. 7–12 Paul is on his way back from Greece to Asia Minor and has sailed away from Philippi after the Passover Feast, and reached the Christians of Troy, and stayed a week there so that he could be sure of meeting them in their gathering on the first day of the week, that is, reckoning Jewish wise, on the Saturday evening. Christians met for an all night session, presumably because some were working round the day, either as slaves or humble freemen, and could only make their adequate observance of the first day of the week by giving up a night's sleep. Luke says, 'Paul talked with them, intending to depart on the morrow'. This is too much for the young man Eutychus, sitting on the windowsill of a crowded third storey room, and he falls asleep and out of the window. Paul is able to recover the young man and then continues the business in hand, and Luke concludes simply, 'And when Paul had gone up and had broken bread and eaten, he conversed with them a long while, until daybreak and so departed. And they took the lad away alive, and were not a little comforted'. Through that window frame out of which Eutychus fell, we have this picture of the member of a small Christian community giving up a night's sleep to keep the first day of the week, not just to look back, but to renew their life in the dying and rising life of Christ through the breaking of bread, and maintain their mission and momentum in a world that clearly needed renewing.

*   *   *   *   *

These New Testament writers offer us some understanding of that possibility of renewal if we look at the basic strands of the traditions they hand on to us. They offer us three main strands: first a strong sense of a real participation in Christ's body and blood in the act of communion, emphasised by 'This' at the beginning of each phrase. Further, it is a relationship with Christ's effective giving of himself against the wrong in the world in commitment to, and trust in, his Father, answered in resurrection to bring the assurance of forgiveness, and the change of the human situation – the blood of the covenant of the sacrifice of Christ whose blood was poured out, 'for many for the forgiveness of sins'. Thirdly, both 'covenant' and 'many' mean that participation in the body and blood of Christ offers closer unity in life together in his body. 'We who are many are one body, for we all partake of one bread'.

These three strands are the basis of all the centuries of thinking about communion that has followed across the centuries. That thinking begins in the New Testament itself, in the Fourth Gospel, where it is not difficult to see that the author is at times providing corrective material, and at other times reflective material, perhaps writing up sermons or meditations on the tradition. Surprisingly he sets the scene for the Last Supper but only describes the feet washing, as an example of humility, and then passes on to the discourses without actually recounting the supper; the reflection on communion comes instead in discussion after the feeding of the five thousand in chapter 6. This may have been to preserve that true Jewish understanding of anamnesis, that it is not looking back at the historical scene in the Last Supper, but bringing that past into the present relationship, to the Christian feeding on Christ. So in the discussion which follows the day after the feeding of the five thousand, Jesus tries to take their thoughts on from the satisfaction of immediate hunger to the food which endures to eternal life. In response to the request, 'Lord, give us this bread always', he said to them, 'I am the bread of life; he who comes to me shall not hunger, and he who believes in me shall never thirst', and he concludes this passage of John 6. 35–51 with 'the bread which I shall give for the life of the world is my flesh, reminding them that for their sustenance they need communion with his dying and rising life, given for the forgiveness and renewal of men and women.

This is driven home with words, 'Truly, truly, I say to you, unless you eat the flesh of the Son of Man and drink his blood, you have no life in you', which produces the reaction, 'This is a hard saying; who can listen to it?' This produces something of an explanation (6.62) 'What if you were to see the Son of Man ascending where he was before? It is the spirit that gives life, the flesh is of no avail; the words that I have spoke to you are spirit and life'. Here is a reflection of the apostles' experience, tallying with that shown in Luke's writings. The strong realistic words of Jesus at the Last Supper must have been a puzzle for those Jewish disciples with their strong sense of the holiness and of the wholeness of the human body, God's creation. They met Jesus risen from the dead, coming and going from time to time, as he willed, apparently quite freely, for he moved with the freedom of the creator. So they were able to accept his being taken from them in the cloud and be sure of his promise that through the activity of the Spirit of God the relationship would be maintained; in the Spirit they found that his words came to life, and they found their relationship with him focused in the breaking of bread, as he had promised.

Those great events of the death and resurrection of Jesus, his

17

ascension and the coming of the spirit provide as it were stepping stones or piers, on which to rest understanding of the meeting with Christ in the breaking of bread, but it is his promise and pledge, 'This is my body, this is my blood', which carried the first Christians and all their followers over. No wonder Paul talked realistically, and Christians have rightly claimed the real presence of Christ; perhaps that should be better put as the real gift of Christ, for certainly there can be no sense of manipulation for it it made possible by the work of the Spirit, and must be met by faith or openness and trust. Furthermore, it is always a gift of Christ for the life of the world, for the forgiveness of sins, for new relationship, which has often been described as the sacrifice of Christ, but perhaps better as the effectiveness of Christ. This is always for the many, to build us together into the body of Christ. It is not surprising that just as Paul passes on from communion to the need for co-operation of Christians in the body of Christ, so John passes on from the Last Supper to the picture of the vine, and the relatedness of Christians to Christ and to one another, a figure from the very source from which the cup of communion is taken. Already in the New Testament pictures crowd in on one another, but offer us great insights into the relationship with Christ to be found in communion, so that Christians can gain further vision from them as the years go on.

3

WHAT THE CHURCH BEGAN TO FIND

It is useful to remember that the deepening thought of the early Christians about the central act of communion which Jesus had given them was worked out against considerable pressure from the pagan and sometimes persecuting world around them. It was certainly not worked out in any ivory tower, in splendid isolation; it had to stand up to the hard facts of life. Just occasionally we can see the interface, and learn what Christian practice looked like from the other side of Roman society.

What did their enthusiasm look like from the other side to Roman society? We are fortunate to have a letter from that scholarly Roman governor, Pliny the Younger, which he wrote to the Emperor Trajan from Asia Minor in 112 A.D. He was asking for further directions about those who had been reported to him as belonging to the illegal sect of Christians. Their practices appeared to him to be harmless. 'They declared that the sum of their guilt or their error only amounted to this, that on a stated day they had been accustomed to meet before daybreak and to recite a hymn among themselves to Christ as though he were a god, and that so far from binding themselves by oath to commit crime, their oath was to abstain from theft, robbery, adultery, and from breach of faith'. The Latin word for oath is 'sacramentum', and it may well be that Pliny had received a garbled account of the eucharist. He was clearly puzzled, and adds without any apparent qualms 'I thought it the more necessary therefore, to find out what truth there was in these statements by submitting two women who were called deaconesses to the torture, but found nothing but a debased superstition carried to great lengths'. Pliny's letter not only provides an interesting external evidence, but a grim reminder that the forces that pressed on Christ would press on his followers.

Pliny's garbled accounts make us wonder how much the way of doing the eucharist varied across those scattered congregations. From the widespread evidence we have, then and later, it looks as though the prayers and orders varied considerably but recognisably. From the early second century people began to put out what was called 'church orders', or primitive books of liturgies and services as examples rather than set form or patterns. One of the earliest of these, the Didache or Teaching of the Twelve Apostles, appears to come from a more out-of-the-way church in Syria in the early decades of the second century. There is a close correspondence with forms of Jewish synagogues: recent finds at Dura-Europos in the Euphrates valley have revealed synagogue prayers, of which the prayers of the Didache are simple adaptations with the insertion of the reference to Jesus Christ. One of the prayers of the Didache gives an evocative picture which opens up a wider vision, which can still shape our minds. 'We thank thee, our Father, for the life and knowledge which thou didst make known to us through Jesus, thy servant. Glory be to thee for ever. As this bread that is broken was scattered upon the mountains, and gathered together, and became one, so let thy Church be gathered together from the ends of the earth into thy kingdom; for thine is the glory and the power through Jesus Christ for ever'.

* * * * *

The second century began the long procession of prayer books; we can trace the development of thinking both about the nature of the eucharist and the way it is done, even while men argued with their persecutors. We have a vivid glimpse of this in the writings of Justin, known as the Martyr, who met his death in 165. Ten years earlier he had written the first defence or 'apology' of Christianity, addressed to the Emperor Antoninus

Pius. He told the Emperor, and us, something about the services which Christians often had to carry on in secret: they contained readings from the apostles, a sermon by the president, prayers, the kiss of peace, the presentation of the bread and cup, followed by the thanksgiving prayer and the administration both given to those who are present, and carried to those who are absent through sickness or imprisonment. Justin writes, 'as by the word of God, Jesus our Saviour was made flesh, and had both flesh and blood for our salvation; so also the food, which was blessed by the prayer of the Word which proceeded from him, and from which our flesh and blood, by assimilation, receives nourishment, is, we are taught, both the flesh and blood of that Jesus who was made flesh'. He then goes on to quote the words of institution. He does not, however, give any fixed form of the prayer for the thanksgiving, only an indication of the ground it covers. The president is expected to make his own prayer; Justin says 'the president in like manner offers up prayers and thanksgiving with all his strength; and the people give their assent by saying Amen'.

It appears that these prayers of the president at the eucharist developed as the Didache indicates from the Berakah or Jewish thanksgiving prayer, said over the wine at the beginning of the Sabbath, and more particularly the special passover form which Jesus would have said at the Last Supper. The form used by the Eastern Syrian Nestorian church in the early centuries is the liturgy of Addia and Mari probably dating from about 200; it follows the same thanksgiving model of the Berakah and does not include the words of institution. But Justin indicates that the Last Supper, and indeed the crucifixion and the resurrection were the pre-supposition of the Christian thanksgiving, and not surprisingly in most places the words of institution became an integral, and indeed, central part of the thanksgiving prayer, and led on to a following section of anamnesis, or calling into the present of the great events of the crucifixion and resurrection, and a request for the action of the Holy Spirit.

We get a significant picture of this development of the thanksgiving prayer in an odd way in an internal dispute of the church in Rome at the beginning of the third century. Hippolytus, a priest who was the most learned theologian in Rome of his time, was very distressed with the choice as bishop in 217 of

21

Callistus, who had begun life as a slave and had been involved in a number of escapades in his youth. Callistus was something of a liberaliser in his doctrine and his treatment of those who wavered under persecution. Hippolytus did not trust him, and separated from him, and took his congregation with him. It was probably for them that he set down on paper his Apostolic Tradition in which he was maybe using some older traditions, but is almost certainly creating some himself. He certainly does not expect every sentence of the eucharist to be in a fixed form; he says, 'But let each pray according to his capacity. If he can pray in a long and solemn prayer, it is good. But if his prayer he prays at modest length, no one may prevent him, provided only that his prayer is orthodox'. However, he says that samples and familiar linking phrases may be useful to enable the congregation to join in the dialogue. He then goes on to provide a whole thanksgiving prayer as a broad hint of what should be considered orthodox. Hippolytus is by no means hidebound, and his prayer has notable depth and width, and opens up new visions. In the opening section he speaks of Jesus who, 'stretched out his hands when he suffered, that he might free from suffering those who believed in you', and he ends, 'Remembering therefore his death and resurrection, we offer you this bread and cup, giving you thanks that you have counted us worthy to stand before you and minister to you as priests. And we beseech you to send your Holy Spirit on the offering of the Holy Church. Gather them together and grant that all who partake of the holy things may be filled with the Holy Spirit for the confirmation of their faith in the truth, that we may laud and glorify you through your Son Jesus Christ, through whom be glory and honour to you, Father and Son with the Holy Spirit, in your holy church, both now and for ever. Amen'.

In spite of his separation, Hippolytus was recognised as one of the great liturgical thinkers of the early Church; his Apostolic Tradition was used as the base for many church orders in the Eastern church, from 4th century Apostolic Constitutions onwards, though it was not taken up in our western sphere until this century. Some of its phrases, particularly those about the Holy Spirit fulfilling the offering of the Church, and gathering the people of God together, have been used in one of the forms of eucharist prayer in the modern Roman Missal, and in one form provided by the Alternative Service Book of the Church of England. For all his difficulties and arguments, Hippolytus proved to be a formative influence.

* * * * *

Behind the arguments of the first centuries lay the struggles of people to find out how God really worked, and not least how God worked through Jesus. The arguments were often vehement even when Christians were living under considerable pressure from persecution which often became violent. The violence rose to a final crescendo with generals making a bid to control the Roman Empire. When Constantine finally established himself he backed Christianity as the religion to unite his empire and made it legal and indeed popular. This produced a new problem for the church, to teach those who flocked into its ranks. It produced some further sets of questions as to how do the things of God work, not only about the person of Christ, but also his sacraments and indeed about Christian life and behaviour. We are fortunate to have the lectures or talks of instruction given to those seeking baptism and membership by Cyril, Bishop of Jerusalem in the middle of the fourth century, at a time when many were considering Christianity for the first time as a serious proposition, and many thousands of pilgrims were flocking to the holy places of Jerusalem. In explaining communion he takes further Hippolytus's simple thought about the Holy Spirit working on the offerings of the Church, and goes on to say, 'Having sanctified ourselves by these spiritual hymns, we call upon the merciful God to send his Holy Spirit on the elements we have set before him, that he may make the bread the body of Christ, and the wine the blood of Christ. For whatever is touched by the Holy Spirit is sanctified and transformed'. Cyril not only introduces the idea of transformation by the Holy Spirit, but also provides us with early evidence of practical advice about receiving communion – 'When you approach . . . make your left hand a throne for your right, which is about to receive your king. Cup your hand to receive the body of Christ and respond, 'amen' . . . Then after partaking of Christ's body, you approach the cup of his blood. Do not stretch out your hands. Bow your head, say 'amen' with adoration and reverence, and sanctify yourself by partaking of Christ's blood also . . . Then wait for the prayer and give thanks to God for counting you worthy of such mysteries'.

Across the Mediterranean a few decades later, a godly provincial governor, Ambrose, was called by public acclaim to become Bishop of Milan. He devoted himself to the study of theology, and not surprisingly became a direct and forceful preacher. He too spoke clearly of the transformation saying, 'through the mystery of the sacred prayer they are transformed into flesh and blood'. The prayer, however, which he quotes as in use at Milan, does not speak of this being done by the Holy Spirit, but just by the quoting of Christ's promise in communion, 'Grant to us that this offering be approved spiritual and acceptable, as the figure of the body and blood of our Lord Jesus Christ, who on the day before he suffered, took bread in his holy hands, looked up into heaven to you Father Almighty, everlasting God. Giving thanks he blessed, broke, and gave the broken bread to his apostles and disciples saying, 'This is my body . . . This is my blood'. It was Ambrose largely who set the pattern of the development of eucharistic prayers in the west, eventually leading to the canon of the Latin mass. It gave the simplest – or perhaps the crudest – explanation of how does it work – by quoting the words of Jesus at the Last Supper. The churches of the eastern Mediterranean however, continued to think of the work of the Holy Spirit in the eucharist and this tradition was preserved in the Orthodox Church; the invocation of the Spirit has now returned to enrich the thinking of most of the modern revisions, including that of Rome itself.

Ambrose's preaching had a large part to play in the conversion to Christianity of a notable young teacher of rhetoric who had come to Milan from North Africa, Augustine. He was in time to become a bishop himself on his return to Africa at Hippo, and to shew himself a greater theologian than Ambrose, perhaps the greatest theologian of the western church. At the same time he preached direct and relatively simple, but highly original, sermons to his congregation in North Africa. 'That bread which you see on the altar, sanctified by the Word of God, is Christ's body. That cup, or rather the contents of that cup, sanctified by the Word of God, is Christ's blood, which He shed for us'. He went on to open up new visions for them, as he did one Easter to those who had just been baptised and confirmed, 'If you want to understand what is meant by "the body of Christ", you must attend to the words of the apostles: "You are the body of Christ and his members, So then, if you are the body of Christ and its members it is the mystery of yourselves that you receive. It is to what you are, that your make the response 'Amen', and in making that response you give your personal assent".'

Augustine is drawing on Paul's picture of Christians as one body in Christ as they feed on his body and the one loaf, and that vision from the Didache. He goes on to enlarge on that text saying, 'as the loaf is composed of many grains which unite in such a way that separate grains cannot be seen at all . . . so we are joined to one another and to Christ . . . if then we are one flesh in the same loaf and actually become the same body, why do we not all show the same love as well, and become one in that respect too?' He made a similar point in his great work 'The City of God' in X.6. 'We are one body in Christ as the Church celebrates in the sacrament of the altar, so well known to the faithful, wherein is shown that in that oblation the Church is offered'.

Like Paul, Augustine wrote against a background of divisions in the Church. He faced a strong Puritan and nationalist sect of the Donatists who kept themselves firmly apart from the rest of Christendom. Yet out of this situation Augustine was able to give Christians this new and vivid picture, 'it is the mystery of yourselves that is placed on the Lord's table, it is to what you are, that you make the response, and in making that response make your personal assent'. This is a challenge not only to Christians in Northern Ireland, which in many ways is so like Augustine's North Africa, but to Christians anywhere in the present divided Church.

4

FACING CONTRADICTIONS

So the church began to find its way, and to help us to find our way to understanding and communion with the Lord. Thus far, up to the 5th century the church looked fairly simple, and the way comparatively plain sailing. It may look very different to us nowadays with a series of different churches with different notice boards, sometimes facing each other across the road; and behind those exteriors some different views, even at its heart about communion, appearing to offer mutually exclusive communions.How do we find the way through all these? We must not be surprised however, that there are differences. Differences of human temperament and circumstances lead to different views, and can lead to serious divergence and division. This is not new, even in the church. You can see Paul facing the divisions within his congregation at Corinth in his letters to them. We have seen Augustine trying to help his communicants to see the unity of Christ's body when they were deeply divided from some of their neighbours, partly due to local nationalism, but also due to divergent views about puritanism.

As thought developed trying to understand Christian experience and faith and worship, so disagreements arose within that faith and worship. We see differences arising as thought develops politically, too. The strength of the faith of the New Testament is shown by the way in which the differences arising in the thought about it keep rubbing up against its strong call to unity through its offer of relationship with the one Christ. The call that Paul made to his Christians back in Corinth has echoed down the centuries. It was heard amongst the different cries of the Reformation, and in the apparent reaction of the 18th century, and again more strongly at the end of the 19th, and into the ecumenical movement of our own century as we have seen parts of the church uniting. The exclusiveness of communion has gradually been broken and the churches, as a whole, are now addressing themselves to a common understanding of baptism, eucharist and ministry. Churches have discovered, as they respond to this call, that it must be putting together the varied insights which have been perceived over the years. In this process we can find help even from the contradictions, not only as they explain the confusion we are faced with today, but as they shew us different insights to put together. We can usefully look at some of these in outline across the centuries.

* * * * *

The church Augustine served in North Africa was to be submerged by the invasion of the Vandals within a few years of his death, and much of the western Roman Empire was to be engulfed in invasions over the succeeding centuries, in what we now call the Dark Ages. Yet the light of Christ was strong enough to work within these invasions and to win over whole nations, very superficially in large parts no doubt, but producing notable Christians within them. Not surprisingly there was much crude teaching of Christian faith and worship, with descriptions of the reality of Christ's presence in communion in terms of blood on the altar. As a result lay folk kept their distance, and tended to worship without communicating. As life settled down and peace became widespread, so the church could become more positive in its pastoral care, and theologians could begin to think systematically about their faith and teaching. The Lateran Council in 1215 had to order all to make their communion at least once a year at Easter, and to make their confession before a priest beforehand. At the same Council the mediaeval church laid down a firmly realist doctrine of the transubstantiation of bread and wine into the body and blood of Jesus. It was later that century that the great Dominican theologian, Thomas Aquinas, set out to explain what this meant in terms of the newly translated metaphysics of Aristotle.

Following Aristotle, Thomas describes all the physical properties of the bread and wine and their outward appearance, as the 'accidents'. The reality or nature of what it is is what he calls the 'substance', and it is this which Aquinas says is changed in the consecration into the body and blood of Christ. Aquinas was in fact trying to save the Church from crude views about the flesh of Christ being broken on the altar and the blood poured out. But refinements are not easy to make clear to the general public, and one result was to give a very localised view about the presence of Jesus, that he is here, and not there. An apparently simple explanation followed, that Jesus is made present by the repetition of the words of institution, and then in prayer of offering which follows, and the breaking of the bread, the priest offers the sacrifice of Jesus on the cross for the sins of the world.

The mediaeval reaction from crudity to awe had led to the giving of communion to the laity in bread only, from the fear that some would drink too much wine. Here again Aristotle's philosophy enabled theologians to say that the change of the substance of the bread and the wine meant that the reality of Christ's body and blood were contained in each of the elements. This looks like a piece of rationalising of a practice which no doubt simplified matters with a large number of communicants, but loses a vivid link not only with the Last Supper, but with the whole thought of Jesus' offering of himself. Often in the past, as in the present, some have come to the table, and then retreated from it in a mixture of fear that it will cost them too much trouble, or that they are not good enough for it. People often rationalise this into listening and worshipping from afar. In the high Middle Ages the elevation of the host became the high point of the service, concentrating on offering the sacrifice of Jesus to the exclusion of communion with him and with one another. 'Heave it higher, Sir Priest' was the cry of the mediaeval Eton scholars.

*   *   *   *   *

It was the New Testament that led Christian thinkers to face the contradictions in this attitude, and led to the movement for reform. Luther's protest was about this distancing man from God; in his studies of St. Paul he rediscovered the openness of

God accepting us in justification by faith in union with Christ. So Luther saw a great point in communion which he saw as the real gift of God in Christ. He held a high view of the reality of Christ given in communion; he was strongly against the symbolic theories of the Swiss reformer Zwingli. He took the alternative mediaeval view of consubstantiation when the reality of Christ is given, while the reality of the bread and wine is maintained. He was concerned that communion should be available for all people in both bread and wine, and with the service in their own language. He was keen that the people should have an opportunity to participate fully in the worship, not least the singing; with his chorales and hymns he opened up a great tradition which for many is now one of the most helpful parts of the church's particpation in worship.

Luther was anxious to avoid any mediaeval idea of repeating the sacrifice of Christ, but we must recognise that in his communion in German he first cut out much of the reference to sacrifice, and then also cut out much of the thanksgiving part. Yet Luther was concerned to provide both the ministry of the word and of the sacrament, and did a great work in opening both up to the people. He was clear that Sunday worship found its focus both in the word and communion. From Luther both German and Scandinavian Lutherans have inherited a service which is a communion service, if it is used in its entirety. That it has not always been so used shows that Luther suffered as others have done, in not always carrying his followers into continuing commitment in practice. But the outline remains and has enabled Lutherans particularly in Scandinavia, to play their part in the movement of renewal of worship in this century.

Where did Calvin stand in worship? Somewhere between Luther and Zwingli, but nearer to Luther, having a great sense of the gift of Christ in communion. His great stress on the transcendence of God made him insist that the words of institution should be thought of as proclaiming the promise of Christ rather than a direct consecration. He saw the receiving of the life of Christ in communion in terms of assurance, sharing in the eternal life, and the forgiveness of sins, if this sacrament is received with faith. His views led him to reconstruct the service further than Luther, and to break up the central act into a series of separate prayers, one section being the simple recital of the words of the institution, as the pledge which makes the sacrament effective. Though this may lead to some simplification, it also loses the thought of the great act, and makes the point of sharing in the act of Christ less obvious. Calvin however himself was clear that the communion should be celebrated at least weekly. The city council at Geneva resisted him and took the easier course, which Zwingli had taken in Zurich, of having communion quarterly. Quarterly and even less frequent communion, had been a common practice for actually receiving communion in the Middle Ages, when people were content to worship from a distance at the elevation, but for the Reformers, no communicating meant no service.

It was the practice, rather than the theology, of Geneva which most influenced Calvinism in its worship as it spread across the Low Countries and beyond. The Scottish Presbyterians inherited one of the purest forms of Calvinism; John Knox, in his Book of Common Order in 1564, reproduced the directions of the English congregation in Geneva. Knox actually assumed that communion would be celebrated monthly, but very soon this was replaced by four communions a year, partly due to the fewness of Reformed ministers available. The great stress of the Reformers on worthy reception led to a very thorough form of preparation for communion in the form of the visitation of the whole of the congregation during the previous week before the communion on Sundays. This produced a number of solemn services, with quarterly opportunities for moral exhortation by elders; it also produced a fine basis of pastoral care for the congregation with a strong corporate sense of communion. This renewed an insight into the mystery of our communion with one another, seen earlier by Paul, by the Didache, and by Augustine, but the much reduced frequency of celebrating greatly reduced its effect.

* * * * *

Cranmer, though reforming in spirit, was not called to be the same sort of Reformation leader as Luther and Calvin. His concern was to produce an English Prayer Book for the English people, and he showed himself a sensitive master of the English language. The same sensitivity made him very alert to criticism and views of others, both Reformers and Catholic bishops, and he showed this right up to the moment of his tragic death. In the first Prayer Book he produced for Edward VI in 1549, the communion service was largely a translation of the Latin Mass, with some abbreviation of the thanksgiving prayer, but containing an anamnesis and offering section in modified form to give the thought of sharing in the offering of Christ. He also included an exhortation and general confession for the people which were similar to some of the more moderate Lutheran forms.

There was, however, a stronger tide of Calvinism flowing into England and a more radical second book was produced in 1552. The consecration prayer was shorn of most of its thanksgiving and its prayer to God for his action, and left with just a brief thanksgiving for redemption and the words of institution. Any commemoration of the offering of Christ with a thought of sharing in it is left to the post-communion prayer. The eucharist vestments of alb and chasuble, which were continued in 1549, were discarded in favour of a surplice, and altars were placed lengthwise in the choir of the church as a table. All this was not enough for some of the Protestant critics; John Knox protested strongly against kneeling to receive. At the last minute, giving heed to this criticism, a special rubric was added in heavy black type at the end of the service explaining that kneeling to receive is a sign of humility and thankfulness and did not imply 'any real and essential presence there being of Christ's natural flesh and blood'.

The Reformation in England owed much to the interest and initiative of its sovereigns, both in its inception and reactions. The 1552 Prayer Book was put away a year later when Mary came to the throne and the Roman Mass was restored. It was brought out again when Elizabeth came to the throne in 1559, but with one or two modifications in words and use which owed much to the Queen's own interests. She had a considerable concern for the importance and dignity of the eucharist; and evidence of this concern was to be found in her own chapels. Though she was content to return to the 1552 form, the 1549 words of administration were added to those of 1552. A rubric was introduced allowing the use of vestments as at the beginning of Edward VI's reign, and the 'black rubric' was omitted. There were further moderating influences in Stuart times. Archbishop Laud ordered altars to be turned east in the churches; Charles I attempted to restore a fuller form of service with the Prayer Book for Scotland in 1637, following the lines of the 1549 service. All this added fuel to the fire to break out in the Civil War and brought the Scottish Covenanters to unite with the English Puritans.

Reaction came again on the restoration of the monarchy in 1660. The Prayer Book revised by Elizabeth in 1559 was restored and the Savoy Conference was called to try to rally all English Christians behind it. It failed to do this but succeeded in producing in 1662 what was to remain the Church of England Prayer Book for 300 years. As a concession to the Puritans the black rubric was put back, but with the words 'corporal presence' instead of 'real and essential presence'. However the rubrics of the book emphasised that the minister of communion must be a priest or ordained by a bishop. As in 1559, the 1662 Prayer Book was seen as a victory for moderation of Christian worship over the Puritans. However, looked at in longer perspective, the moderates were much closer to the Puritans than they realised. The communion service of 1662 bears many marks of its reduction in its central prayer, with that brief thanskgiving for redemption leading straight on to the words of institution. This does not do justice to the Christian and Jewish tradition of thanking God for all his work. It turns the words of institution into a formula, and does not express what the prayer is really trying to do; it only mentions the death of Christ, and not his resurrection or ascension or the gift of the Spirit. The Church of England is certainly fortunate in that Cranmer was a master of the English language at a time when the Elizabethan writers had forged it into a fine tool. Yet this good fortune delayed many generations from stopping to think of what Christians are really doing in the eucharist.

*   *   *   *   *

It may seem strange that after all the turmoils and changes of the previous hundred odd years, the Prayer Book should remain unchanged for the next 300 years. The quick answer perhaps is to say that the Church went to sleep for at least half that period. Of course this is an exaggeration, but it is not surprising that men reacted to the religious violence of the 16th and early 17th centuries and wanted a rest. Devotion certainly lessened, and with it appreciation of the eucharist. Celebrations were reduced to quarterly intervals and vestments were put away. But this situation of torpor was just the one to fire the teaching of the Wesleys. Even at the end of the 1720's, John and Charles Wesley and George Whitfield were members of the 'Holy Club', who normally had communion weekly. John, with his brother Charles, had a high doctrine of the sacrament, and of Christ's presence and acts within it, and this was further strengthened by his conversion experience in 1738. It was in fact partly to provide his fellow Methodists with opportunity for the sacrament that thirty years later John Wesley began to ordain ministers first in America and then in England.

One of the greater contributions of the Wesleys was through their hymns. It is significant the number of hymns they wrote about the eucharist. Some of the best known are lines of John –

> Author of life divine,
> Who hast a table spread
> Furnished with mystic wine
> And everlasting bread.

Charles has some very striking verses setting out both the reality and the objectivity of the sacrament, and also the supernatural wonder.

> We need not now go up to heaven
> To bring the long-sought Saviour down;
> Thou are to all already given,
> To every faithful soul appear
> And show thy real Presence here.

and

> Angels in fixed amazement
> Around our altars hover,
> With eager gaze adore the grace
> Of our eternal lover;
> Himself and all his fulness
> Who gives to the believer;
> And by this bread whoe'er are fed
> Shall live with God for ever.

The Wesleys and Whitfield produced a chain reaction of further revivals, the first among evangelicals within the Church of England and Wales. A further reaction to this came in the 40's of the 19th century with the movement of those in Oxford who discovered the excitement of the historic and catholic heritage of the Church of England, and produced 'Tracts for the Times'. The third of these powerful pamphlets was entitled 'Thoughts on Alterations in the Liturgy', and a later one by Pusey 'On the Holy Eucharist'. As it turned out, the Tractarians did not press for alterations in the Prayer Book at this stage. Pusey and Liddon were content to celebrate in surplice and scarf, using the Prayer Book service. It was the second and third generation of Tractarians who revived the eucharistic vestments, and began to say the prayer of offering, put as a thanksgiving in 1662, at the end of the consecration prayer as in 1549, and to use the Lord's Prayer before communion. But the real alteration the Tractarians brought about was to remind the 19th century Church and its successors, that communion is the centre of the Christian worship. They did a great service to the Church in doing this, and it was no easy one to carry out in the circumstances that they found. The Prayer Book had envisaged Sunday worship consisting of a preparatory act of morning prayer, followed by the litany leading on into communion, with the service most likely sung. This remained the order on the few sacrament Sundays of the 18th century at the festivals and quarters. On other Sundays the service ended with the first part of the communion and the antecommunion. When Wesley and other reformers wanted more frequent communion, and with a high sense of preparation, to encourage fasting communion, they rose to do it early in the morning. The Tractarians were concerned to replace the truncated form of mattins, litany, and ante-communion by a splendid celebration of communion as a main act of worship each Sunday. If this was to occupy the centre of Sunday morning after breakfast, then people must be encouraged to communicate at a said celebration before breakfast, and then return to a sung celebration to worship which would have as the sole communicant the priest.

In a strange way the 18th and 19th centuries revivals had returned to the strongly individualistic Christianity which had grown up in the later Middle Ages, so this split of eucharistic worship did not seem so odd, and a considerable number responded to this call, particularly in the towns. It also brought a considerable revival of week-day celebrations. Dean Hook, while still vicar of Leeds, took the first step of instituting evening celebrations to meet the needs of those working in factories who started too early to get to morning celebrations. This brought criticism from one quarter, but was soon followed by the Roman Catholics. It was noted also that Tractarian clergy threw themselves particularly into slum parishes and produced a warm response and colourful eucharistic worship. Colours and lights all helped, but only because men and women found through these God in Jesus inviting them to meet with him and receive his life, the life that Jesus shared from the carpenter's bench to the cross. All this pointed the need to recover a service of corporate worship, and moreover a worship that was related to the working world. There was more for the Church to find out about sharing its worship one with another, and about making a whole of it, and a whole of life.

5

FINDING A WAY THROUGH

When arguments have gone on for some time, apparently at cross purposes, it is often a simple statement of a familiar truth that brings people back to the point to find a way through. So it seems to have been with Christian worship; its course, through the Middle Ages, the Reformation, on into the 19th century revivals, seems to have been one of piling up oversimplified and overemphasised views of one kind or another, to set word against sacrament, priest against people, God against the world. Where was the way through to be found?

The answer came from what might have seemed to be an unlikely source, the Roman Catholic Church; the roots of revival were laid in what must have seemed a bastion of the old world, the Benedictine Abbey of Solesmes. This produced notable thought and work about worship in the middle of the 19th century. This work became a world-wide concern of the Roman Church through the simple statement of Pius X; in one of his first encyclicals as Pope in 1903 he said 'to restore the true Christian spirit, the faithful must be brought back to the first and indispensable source of that spirit, the active participation of the faithful in the holy mysteries'. Recall to 'active participation in the holy mysteries' sounds surprisingly obvious, now, but in effect was a recall to reality for many Christians from distant non-communicating worship. The call was spelt out in some effective work either side of the first World War on the part of a number of Benedictine Abbeys. Abbot Herwegen of Maria Laach in the Rhineland pointed out that Christian worship must be our response to God's action in Christ, which realises the divine in the human; our worship becomes the lifting up of our humanity to God. The eucharist is our way of taking part in the saving work of Christ; Christianity is not a doctrine but a life.

The teaching work which originated from these Benedictine Abbeys spread far, not only to the Roman Church, but across the Churches; it set going a whole liturgical movement. It began simply in the congregation actually making the responses in the service. This was a very obvious picking up of the point of the Reformers, but by the 18th century even many Reformed services had lapsed into only a clerk making the responses. This participation in word would lead much further, and eventually lead Roman Catholics to return to celebrating communion in the vernacular languages, and to the earlier practice of the priest standing behind the altar facing the people. Immediately Pius X's encyclical led to more frequent communion and helped the movement back to weekly communion, and to the use of week-days too. This influence was soon spread wider to Lutheran churches particularly in Germany and Scandinavia. Friedrich Heiler in Germany and Yngve Brilioth in Sweden were notable pioneers and writers whose books soon found their way to England and into translation, in the 1920's.

*　　*　　*　　*　　*

Not surprisingly for England the most significant step bringing Christian worship back into focus was one which concerned the times of services. Time is of course a very practical matter for all people, not least for Christian congregations. Many congregations have been and still are, split between those who come at 8 a.m. and those who come at 11 a.m. The way forward lay in the simple step of a celebration with the majority communicating, generally with the singing largely congregational, starting sometime between 8.45 a.m. and 10.30 a.m. and often followed by a communal breakfast or refreshments. By its communal aspects it took the name of the parish communion. In many ways it was a very obvious move to make, but so often obvious moves take some time to discover and have to wait for another period for any one to undertake them. The first parish to

37

undertake this in England was a rural parish in Warwickshire, Temple Balsall, which did so in 1913 under its vicar, F. R. Fairbairn. He thought it offered a reconciliation between 8 a.m. and 11 a.m. not only in times, but also in attitude to communion. It also offered to those who were used to an early communion and a later mattins a way of putting word and sacrament together. A later start was a help to those who rose early every other day of the week, to come and join in communion, and so brought together whole families, young and old. The refreshment afterwards provided an opportunity for members of the congregation who might have worshipped previously at different times, to meet one another, and so to become conscious of themselves as a body of Christians and in fact, the body of Christ in that place. Fairbairn wrote later in terms similar to those of Herwegen, 'If we are to stem the tide of this individualistic religion still prevalent among Church people . . . we must remind ourselves again and again that the Christian religion is a sacramental religion . . . This essentially corporate character of Christianity lies in the fact that the Christian society, the Church, is the Body of Christ: that individual membership in it consists in a relationship, a living contact of one with another, and with our Lord Himself, within the one Body'.

The parish communion movement gradually spread through its practical appeal as well as its theological, encouraged by literature from the liturgical movement coming over from the Continent and further English contributions. Churches in towns followed the example of the country parish in the 20's and 30's. Beginning from sharing times of services, congregations went on to discover the further point of their shared life in the body of Christ, sharing his work, in his offering for the sake of the world.

* * * * *

A good deal of attention of Anglican church people in the 1920's and of the general public had been focused on trying to revise the prayer Book. A Royal Commission, appointed in 1904, had reported two years later that the Book of Common

Prayer was too narrow for the Church of the 20th century. The Church had started the process of revision in 1906, but moved slowly with an interruption by the war. Much of the argument was about producing a more satisfactory communion service, not least its central prayer of thanksgiving and consecration. It was hoped this could contain the wide diversity of use which had grown up between the Catholic and Evangelical elements in the Church of England. As the law stood then the only way to revise the service was to get an act through Parliament to authorise the revised Prayer Book. Though in the Convocations of the Church a substantial majority was able to agree on the revision, the two wings on either side were strong enough and prepared to combine to lobby parliamentary opinion to reject the revised book on two occasions in 1927 and 1928. The consecration prayer included a petition to the Spirit 'to bless and sanctify both us and thy gifts of bread and wine, that they may be unto us the body and blood of thy son our Saviour Jesus Christ'. This was too direct a prayer for consecration for the evangelicals, and in those days too like the eastern Orthodox for the catholic wing. The rejection of the book by Parliament after the Church bodies passed it, raised considerable problems for many about relations of Church and State, but the forces of reconciliation were strong enough to deal with this; bishops used their discretion in the use of many alternatives provided in the revised book and a fair amount of it passed into general use. The Church found that this way of proceeding was not really the best way for liturgical revision, but it took another thirty years to produce and get through Parliament a Measure allowing the Church to use alternative services for trial periods, and later to produce an alternative book. Much of the 1928 material passed into the first series of alternative services in 1966. More usefully the Church also learnt that there had been insufficient thought about worship at the time the material was prepared for the Prayer Book; the insights of the liturgical movement had not been drawn upon by that stage. The Church of England needed to benefit by further thinking before it could move towards a new book.

That further thinking can be sampled in two particlar books on worship written in the 30's and 40's; just as the liturgical movement on the Continent sprang out of the work of monastic communities, so these two books came out of two Anglican communities. A notable contribution in the thirties was the book *Liturgy and Society* written by Gabriel Hebert of the Kelham Community in 1935. Though it now seems a very church-centred book, it was one of the first in English to give expression to the worship of the church as sharing in the offering of Christ for the world. Hebert was very much indebted to the Continental liturgical movement amongst Catholics and Lutherans; he took up from them their concern for the lifting up of all life to God, and its expression in art and architecture. He was also conscious that he was writing against the background of mounting European crisis. In a concluding paragraph he wrote 'In these days of anxiety and fear and impending tribulation, Christians have their witness to bear, of the reality of God; of the dignity of man, called to be a child of God, so that the bodily life even of the lowest has an eternal meaning; and of the vocation of the Church to express in her worship and the common life of her members the pattern of the foundations of the City of God'.*

The other notable book was *The Shape of the Liturgy* by Dom Gregory Dix, a member of the Anglican Benedictine Community at Nashdom. This appeared at the end of the war in 1945, just ten years after Hebert's *Liturgy and Society*. *The Shape of Liturgy* was a large book and had much to say in the way of history and theology. As with Hebert some of this now appears dated. Its major contribution lay in the thought behind its title 'The Church took from the Last Supper the four-fold shape – he took, he gave thanks, he broke, and he gave'. In directing attention to this simple shape, Dix helped people to see that the eucharist is something done rather than said; he took people's attention away from concentration on particular elements, and helped them to see the whole process of 'doing' the eucharist as one of joining in the eternal act of Christ. Dix would probably have been surprised at the extent and the particular way in which his thoughts on the shape of the liturgy were to contribute to the process of the reform of the eucharist in the renewal of worship.

* A. G. Hebert Liturgy and Society London 1935.
† Gregory, Dix – The Shape of the Liturgy London 1945.

The particular route by which this came was, to the surprise of some, through the United Church of South India, which in 1947 brought together the episcopal Anglican church with non-episcopal Free churches. Anglicans in this country were very tentative about this step, but within a few years, not only Anglicans but Roman Catholics came to admire the new communion service which the Liturgical Committee of the United Church produced in 1950. It brought together a good deal of material from the Anglican Prayer Book and also material from Free Church Orders, and furthermore from liturgies of the Orthodox Church in India. It was the first communion service to make clear in its central thanksgiving prayer the four-fold shape of taking and giving thanks, breaking and giving; it also spelled out clearly the sections of the other parts of the service. It gave full provision for congregational participation; it introduced acclamations at the end of the words of institution, and a further acclamation following the remembrance or anamnesis section, leading on to a prayer for the Holy Spirit. The Lord's Prayer follows, then the breaking of bread. It spelt out the process of the eucharist, and enabled all members of the congregration to feel they were doing it. As a young expatriate girl remarked to her mother, 'It is much better; it's not just the clergyman, it's all of us'. It was all of us in another sense too, of combining catholic and evangelical traditions, and presented a major step forward which could probably only have been made with the accompanying step of church unity. It was to prove in many ways the pioneer of revisions of the eucharist for the second half of the 20th century.

Some of these results happened through the direct personal contact of Dr. Leslie Brown, who was the first secretary of the South India Liturgical Committee. In 1953 he was to become Bishop, and later Archbishop, of Uganda. In the early 60's he was in charge of the production of a Liturgy for Africa for the use of all Anglicans there. This follows the South India lines, but uses some new material in the thanksgiving after communion. Dr. Brown was also to take a leading part in discussions on liturgical revision across the Anglican communion through two Lambeth Conferences. At the 1968 conference the task of preparing a document on the basic structure of the eucharist was given to him and Dr. Ronald Jasper, who was already beginning the process of revision in the Church of England as chairman of the Liturgical Commission.

The Church of South India also gave careful attention to the first part of the eucharist in the introduction and ministry of the word. It took up the primitive tradition of three readings from the Old Testament, Epistle and Gospel, with the sermon to follow directly after the Gospel. Then the Creed sums up this section and is followed by the intercessions which also makes opportunity for responses and litany forms. All this was in itself a recovery of more of the fullness of Christian worship, but it was a further help to Christians in the evangelical tradition both to see that the ministry of the word was fully provided for, and also to find that all this is completed in the ministry of the sacrament, as the word passes into action. This drawing together of word and sacrament was to spread in both directions; the Roman Catholic Church was to reinstate the sermon or homily as part of the order of Mass in the reform stemming from Vatican II. Both the Methodists and Congregationalists in this country were to present their revised liturgies in the form of one Sunday service, of word and sacrament, as in the revisions in the Church of England. This drawing together helped those who had divided their worship into two parts of communion and mattins, or a preaching service, to put them together, and very often to put two congregations together. Any change in human affairs which affects us deeply is often painfully slow, but the first sixty years of this century had gone some way to help Christians find their way through the contradictions.

6

FINDING THE WORDS

When you probe into life you find a lot of things are connected up and hang together. This is very true of the human body; disorder in one part upsets the whole, and fortunately too, a dose or application in one part can right the whole. This is true of the whole of life related to God. So Paul discovered that Christians were in a relationship with Christ, as limbs of a body, and that body was built up by feeding on the body and blood of Christ in communion. He realised too, that this called for real unity and clear thinking about communication with God, and with fellow Christians. Paul in his time had to press these points particularly against those who were over-enthusiastic about displaying their life in the Spirit in unintelligible tongues.

The Reformers pressed for this clear communication by translating the Bible and services into their native tongues from the old Latin. Cranmer wrote in the second introductory section of the Prayer Book under the title *Concerning the Service of the Church*, 'St. Paul would have such language spoken to the people in the church that they might understand and have profit by hearing the same'. But the Reformers were so keen on pressing their points that they sometimes overlooked the need for unity.

The 20th century has found its conscience pressed by the need for unity, and the first full fruit of this in the United Church in South India brought attention back to provision for that unity in communion. At the same time the Church found itself pressed by another need to take the Scriptures with fresh seriousness arising from the Bible and biblical theology. This in turn produced new translations of the Scriptures in contemporary language. These two pressures combined to produce concern to find the contemporary words in which to express the worship of the Church in communion.

This movement gained much momentum to lead to action in the 1960's all across the Church, not only in this country but also in the U.S.A. and Europe, and across the Roman Catholic communion. Various bodies for revising liturgies started at that time – the second Vatican Council's liturgical considerations, and the Church of England Liturgical Commission, and committees in the Methodist and Congregational Churches. The joint Liturgical Group in this country, combining Anglicans, Free Churches with observers from the Church of Scotland and the Roman Catholics began in this period. The Church of England, learning from its experience in 1928, was able to get through Parliament the Alternative Services Measure in 1965, and in 1974, after another move had gathered its governing bodies in one General Synod of clergy and laity, secured a Worship and Doctrine Measure. These have allowed the Church to try out provisional forms of services for a period, and then to make its own arrangements about revised services as alternatives within the agreed framework of the doctrine of the 39 Articles, and the Book of Common Prayer. This enabled the Church to set going some revision of order and wording of the communion service. This began in Series II in 1967. The extended thanskgiving prayer took up the material of the Prayer Book, and added to it a stronger prayer for the activity of the Spirit, a recalling of Christ's work, the thought of sharing in the offering, and so helped to restore the feeling of completeness. A greater assistance to many was the clear lay-out of the sections of the service, and the increase of participation by the congregation, particularly the breaking up of the intercessions into sections with responses. The return of the gloria to the opening section strengthened the thought of worship at the beginning of the service. A very much simplified form of confession was a relief to many, if later found to be too simple.

The marking out of different sections provided some encouragement to use different parts of the church for different parts of the service, lectern and pulpit for the ministry of the word, the prayer desk or some part of the nave for intercessions, then a

move to the altar at the offertory for thanksgiving. Many
congregrations have found that these moves have helped them
both to maintain their attention, and to appreciate the action of
the service and its movement. Even simple physical movements
can help human beings to share in eternal actions. Many of the
rubrics or directions in Series II were put in the form of 'may'
giving a choice to congregations to try different ways to
make some sort of experiment. The Liturgical Commission
hoped that congregations would try various ways at different
times. On the whole congregations tended to opt for one choice
and to keep to it, but there was a mixture of experience across
the country. This was gathered up by an extensive questionnaire
which was circulated after the service have been in use for two
years. The experiences in use revealed in the completed question-
naires were used in the preparation of the Series III liturgy
which appeared in 1973.

The movement which started with the Roman Church had
spread not only to Anglicans, but also to Free Churchmen. A
joint liturgical group had been formed between Anglicans and
Free Churches, together with the Church of Scotland and an
observer from the Church of Rome, as far back as 1963, and
had published a volume of essays *Renewal of Worship* in 1965,
and then material about the lectionary. The work of this group
stimulated thought in many churches; one notable revision was
that produced by the Congregational Church in 1970, which
passed into the use of the United Reformed Church at the union
in 1973 with the English Presbyterians. Its Sunday service
brought together word and sacrament in the one service, with
the ministry of the word in the traditional manner of the ante-
communion, followed by the communion. It provides six
different forms of thanskgiving; some of these are set out in the
traditional reformed way of the words of institution first
separately, and then what is in effect a series of separate short
prayers. Others present a picture of the complete action of
thanskgiving, institution, remembrance, offering. The fifth form
puts this specifically 'as we offer thee this bread and cup; we pray
thee to grant through thy Holy Spirit, that we who share in this
holy communion, be united as one body in Christ, may be
renewed in strength and for thy service, and may rejoice in the
life of thy kingdom'. The Revised Methodist Sunday Service

45

providing sections for both ministry of word and ministry of sacrament, indicates that the full Sunday service should include both. Its Thanksgiving Prayer is put briefly, but its final section expresses wide thoughts of offering and unity – 'Grant that by the power of the Holy Spirit we who receive your gifts of bread and wine may share in the body and blood of Christ. Make us one body with him. Accept us as we offer ourselves to be a living sacrifice, and bring us with the whole creation to your heavenly kingdom'. These forms show an interesting picture of the revival of Christian tradition and widening of thought from the Reformation, to make a more complete picture.

Across the Atlantic the Episcopal Church of the United States produced Services for Trial Use in 1971, and then its revised edition of The Book of Common Prayer in 1976. This provided for alternative communion services, Rite I in a fairly traditional form, Rite II a moderate revision using 'you' language. It also goes on to provide an outline 'Order for Celebrating the Holy Eucharist' 'not intended for use at Sunday services', but for weekdays services either in churches or houses, set out in stages required for the central act of Christian worship – 'The people and priest – gather in the Lord's name – proclaim and respond to the word of God – pray for the world and the church – exchange the peace – prepare the table – make eucharist – break the bread – share the gifts of God', and gives some useful suggestions under each section, and some shorter forms of eucharistic prayers. The main Rite II provides a selection of eucharistic prayers with varying emphasis. Prayer C has a notably wide Thanksgiving for creation and the human race, and the course of redemption, and a concluding section of offering. It manages to bring together the reformed and subjective conclusions of the Prayer of Humble Access into the objective traditional prayer of offering, 'Deliver us from the presumption of coming to this table for solace only, and not for strength; for pardon only, and not for renewal. Let the grace of this Holy Communion make us one body, one spirit in Christ, that we may worthily service the world in his name'.

Meanwhile, the Roman Catholic Church across the world had been making its revisions arising out of the sessions of the Second Vatican Council. The Constitution on Sacred Liturgy which issued from the Council in 1963 gave as its aim 'full active participation by the people demanded by the very nature of the liturgy'. The most immediate result of this was the production of translations of the liturgy in the vernacular. This produced a variety of different translations in different English-speaking countries. Fortunately an international committee for English in the Liturgy (ICEL) was formed. Meanwhile a Commission had been appointed to produce a revised order of the Mass, which it did in 1970, and standard English texts were produced of this. The 1970 Mass included four possible forms of the eucharistic prayer; the first was the old Roman canon complete with intercession in the first half, and prayers for the departed and commemoration of the saints following the oblation. This itself was couched in the strong sacrificial terms which had given rise to Protestant fears about thoughts of repeating Christ's sacrifice. The other three new forms moved away from the conglomerate form of prayer, leaving just a short intercession in the earlier part of the service. The three new forms of thanksgiving moved in line with modern Roman Catholic thought of sharing in the sacrifice, 'Lord look upon this sacrifice you have given to your Church and by your Holy Spirit gather all who share in this one bread and one cup into one body of Christ, a living sacrifice of praise', as the last of the forms puts it. This form draws heavily on the eucharistic prayer of Hippolytus.

In 1974 three further forms were approved, suitable for children's masses.

* * * * *

In 1969 the Roman Catholics Consultation on English in the Liturgy joined with those considering this subject in the Anglican and Lutheran communions and others, to make an ecumenical international consultation on English texts (ICET). This proceeded to work out translations of the texts shared by the congregation and choir in the eucharist, the gloria, creed, sanctus, benedictus and agnus, and the Lord's Prayer. These were published in England under the title *Prayers we have in Common*. They all addressed God as 'you' and provided a basis for all the further revisions of the eucharist in the different

47

churches. One of the great discoveries for people in this process of revision is a discovery of how similar the order of the eucharist of the different churches, Roman Catholic, Anglican, Methodist for instance, are to one another now. This gives a vivid awareness that we are part of a wide and indeed world-wide family. On the other hand, it is still difficult for churches to leave the task of revision to a small representative group as it has to be when meeting representatives of other churches. As a result, each of the churches felt free to make minor alterations in for instance the text of the Lord's Prayer. This may be fair enough if kept within limited proportions, but it has been something of a loss to go back on the agreement worked out by ICET. These texts give a sense of common worship, which can lead on to further mutual understanding of the service and of what is being done in it. A further stage was reached in 1985 with the setting up of ELLC – the English Language Liturgical Consultation.

A notable piece of work on this further understanding has been done by the Anglican/Roman Catholic International Commission (ARCIC). In 1971 it published an agreed statement on the eucharist. The statement acknowledges that there is 'a variety of theological approaches within both our communions'. It shows there has been a remarkable drawing together of understanding both over the questions of sacrifice and presence. Many Christians may be surprised to learn this; they need to read the text of this statement and they will not only find a remarkable agreement but also useful simple explanations of these principal thrusts of Christian worship.

On sacrifice the statement says 'There can be no repetition of or addition to what was then accomplished once for all by Christ . . . The eucharistic memorial is no mere calling to mind of a past event or of its significance, but the church's effectual proclamation of God's might acts . . . In the eucharistic prayer the church continues to make a perpetual memorial of Christ's death, and his members, united with God and one another, give thanks for all his mercies, entreat the benefits of his passion on behalf of the whole church, participate in these benefits and enter into the movement of his self-offering'.

About the presence of Christ in the eucharist, the statement goes on 'Christ is present and active, in various ways, in the entire eucharistic celebration. It is the same Lord who through the proclaimed word invites his people to his table, who through his minister presides at the table, and who gives himself sacramentally in the body and blood of his paschal sacrifice. It is the Lord present at the right hand of the Father, and therefore transcending the sacramental order, who thus offers to his church, in the eucharistic signs, the special gift of himself . . . The Lord's words at the Last Supper, 'Take and eat; this is my body', do not allow us to dissociate the gift of the presence and the act of sacramental eating. The elements are not mere signs; Christ's body and blood become really present and given in order that, receiving them, believers may be united in communion with Christ the Lord'.

It is significant that the references in the report to the third aspect of communion, of sharing life in Christ, do not appear under such a specific heading, but in the first section on the mystery of the eucharist it says, 'Christ through the Holy Spirit in the eucharistic builds up the life of the church, strengthen its fellowship and furthers its mission . . . When we gather around the same table in this communal meal at the invitation of the same Lord and when we 'partake of the one loaf', we are one in commitment not only to Christ and to one another, but also to the mission of the church in the world'. The Commission was inhibited from setting out this aspect more clearly by the fact that this statement itself highlights the anomaly of Christians agreeing in statements but not in communicating together. The Commission recognised that the problems are interlocked, and has gone on from the statement on the eucharist to those on ministry and authority. There are many places on the Continent, and a few in England, where Roman Catholics share communion with Anglicans and others; it should not surprise Roman Catholics that Anglicans press, on the basis of the agreed statement, for the Roman Church to make an official move towards sharing in communion.

*   *   *   *   *

The process of revising services has produced a great cross fertilisation within the churches. Fortunately it had been recognised at the outset that the first revision put forward must be regarded as experimental and therefore, to be tested and monitored, and revised further. In the Church of England a questionnaire was widely circlated on Series II to help towards the preparation of Series III. Meanwhile the Church of Scotland produced a further revision of its Divine Service, and the Methodist Church produced its Sunday Service. All these took up the international texts addressing God as 'you'. When Series III was published in 1973 the 'you' form appeared to be the greatest change to some, but to many more it appeared to be a natural step. Both this and the fact that the service was strengthened in various aspects brought more congregations to realise that the time had come to move to the alternative service. The acclamations between sections of the thanksgiving prayer gave a full opportunity for the congregation to participate and also a help to mark the components for prayer. The opening thanksgiving section was filled out, as were the memorial and offering sections 'We celebrate and proclaim his perfect sacrifice made once for all upon the cross, his resurrection from the dead, and his ascension into heaven; and we look for his coming in glory. Accept through him, our great high priest, this our sacrifice of thanks and praise; and as we eat and drink these holy gifts in the presence of your divine majesty, renew us by your Spirit, inspire us with your love, and unite us in the body of your Son, Jesus Christ our Lord'. These phrases opened up wider thoughts going back to Augustine and quickly made an impression on the minds of congregations, as further reviews have shown. Alongside them we can set the words of the Methodist Sunday Service, 'Make us one body with him. Accept us as we offer ourselves to be a living sacrifice, and bring us with the whole creation to your heavenly kingdom'.

The different churches have always looked forward, from the revision of the eucharist, and the revision of other services, to the production of whole revised prayer books. This has been particularly significant for Anglicans for whom the Book of Common Prayer has been one of the principal unifying features of the Church. It soon became clear, however, that the aim would be not to replace the Book of Common Prayer, but to set beside it another book of revised services for this end of the 20th century, which in time would be replaced by a further revision.

The present revised book was therefore given the name of The Alternative Service Book 1980. It was appreciated that many were waiting for the publication of a complete Alternative Service Book as a time for moving towards a revised use. The point was therefore made that it should include as many options as possible. It also contains readings for a great number of feasts and occasions with alternatives, resulting in a fatter volume than the Roman and American revised books.

A plea was early made to have alternative forms of the thanksgiving prayer of the communion. At first the Bishops declined to accept a proposal from the Liturgical Commission for this, but in subsequent revision debates it was agreed to provide alternatives. This provision is not so complicated as it sounds. The first is the Series III prayer, the second is largely the Series II form, and the fourth the Series I prayer, both in 'you' language. The third prayer as it stands is a new composition, but draws both on the prayer of Hippolytus and on the fourth of the revised Roman Catholic forms. It draws on Hippolytus in the opening thanksgiving section; 'He opened wide his arms for us on the cross; he put an end to death by dying for us, and revealed the resurrection by rising to new life; so he fulfilled your will and won for you a holy people'. It does so again in the concluding section 'Send the Holy Spirit on your people and gather into one in your kingdom all who share this one bread and one cup, so that we, in the company of all the saints, may praise and glorify you for ever'.

The revised form also includes in the appendix a 'you' form of the 1662 consecration prayer. It provides other alternatives, such as for the confession, in an appendix. It provides for the penitential section in two alternative places, at the beginning or after the intercession. In its further provision of Rite B, a combination of the older 'thou' form of the Series I and II orders, the book offers to Anglicans and others an opportunity to follow various well-tried usages in the same book, so that some who have been used to one may sometimes try another.

A majority of Christians nowadays can unite in addressing God as 'you'. This, in fact, is a logical application of the argument that Cranmer presses in the prefaces of the original Prayer Book, that worship should be in the language used and understood by the people. To speak to a person as 'thou' in

English is no longer a sign of affection, rather one of archaism or sarcasm, neither of which we should wish to apply to God. The same applies to the use of shorter sentences rather than the long periodic sentences used by Cranmer; those now belong to the world of the law court or the state, which are not suitable parallels to the courts of heaven or the Church. To this reply is sometimes made that modern language removes all the mystery from the service. This is quite false. If people will take the challenge of the direct language, to read it and to understand it, they will find they are invited into greater mystery. Those who are carried away by the language of Cranmer are carried not into mystery but into mystification. The more understandable words bring us to face the long vista of the renewal of life in Christ, of worshipping in the presence of God, of being a living temple to his glory; we are asked to do more theology rather than less. The book which we put into people's hands today must have a theology for the whole people of God, not just for a limited number of professionals. This is why it is expressed in understandable language and speaks rather more often of participation. The words now invite us to understand the stages of worship, so that we realise that it is not just words but action. They ask us to see that the heart of worship is the eucharistic action of the body of Christ in each place renewing its life in Christ to share in his offering to the Father, to do his work in the world.

7

FINDING YOUR WAY

The same question faces revisers of liturgies as faces mountain climbers – was the first effort worth it? Where does it get you? And the same answer comes back: if the weather is good for the climber, and the revision well done for the worshipper, you get a wonderful, clearer, wider view. The revision of church services has certainly helped people to think about them, and not least to think about their shape and their component parts. So over the last thirty years people have thought more carefully about the four-fold shape of the heart of Christian worship, stemming from the Lord's Supper. The simple, but growing use of sub-titles and clear divisions of parts of the service, has helped many to think more widely and more clearly about the whole shape of Christian worship.

That shape is response to God made known to us in Jesus Christ. We respond to God humbly, but trustfully and thankfully. We take in what he has shown us of himself both in the Old Testament, and in the New, particularly in the gospels. We respond both by confessing our faith and also by confessing our sins and claiming his forgiveness. We share our concerns with him in our intercessions. But we don't stop there, as unfortunately some Christians have done. Christianity is not just a religion of listening and following; it tells us of God who shared our life in Christ and offers to share his life with us. Through the death and resurrection of Christ and the continued working of the Spirit, he shares his dying and rising life with us in the sacrament he gave us in the breaking of bread. We claim this humbly and thankfully as we take the bread and wine to share in his offering of himself; in his strength we go out from this table to offer ourselves in service to God. This is the distinctive pattern of Christian worship, not just to hear God, as one heard from a distance, but to share his life, and his strength to go out with him.

Full Christian worship involves both the ministry of the word and the ministry of the sacrament. These are not two unconnected things, but each contributes to the other. The ministry of the word prepares the ground for the ministry of the sacrament, and gives it meaning and application. The ministry of the sacrament brings the ministry of the word to a point of commitment and communion, of giving and receiving; without it, much Christian faith remains diffuse and undirected. The eucharist has these two main parts, but each of these falls into various further parts. In the revised liturgy we can see the shape of the whole service most simply in seven sections. The first is the preparation section with the sentence, greeting, collect of purity, which may be followed by the penitential section, and by the Kyrie or gloria, and is gathered up in the collect for the day. Then the ministry of the word follows with the readings; these may be three or two, from the Old Testament, epistle and gospel. This is expounded in the sermon, and gathered up in the creed, the summary of the Word. The next section was originally called the prayers. This is primarily the intercessions, but may be followed by the penitential section and then the prayer of humble access as an appropriate end to the first part of the service looking towards the sacrament. The second part of the service can be divided into four parts. The first is the offertory, beginning with the greeting of the peace and followed by the preparation of the vessels. Then follows the eucharistic prayer or thanksgiving with its sections of thanksgiving, memorial, and offering with the prayer for the Spirit. Communion follows, introduced by the Lord's Prayer, and the breaking of the bread, with maybe the Agnus before or accompanying the distribution. Finally there is the section after communion with the post-communion prayer, then the blessing and final greeting.

The sections follow on one another logically enough, but more than that, they do so dynamically. Besides seeing the shape of the sections of the service it is important to see its dynamic nature. Though many would say they come to Church, and particularly to communion, to find the still centre of the week, they need to remember that the still centre is a positive act of worship with a movement of its own, which asks us to move with it. The movement of the different sections can be pictured very simply on the pattern of the steps into church, up to the altar and back again. The preparation is in a sense the doormat for cleaning, the ministry of the word is the porch where we take in the information and the lesson for the week. At the doorway we look round at the world both inside the church and outside to gather them into our prayers. Then we humbly go forward to take our offering of bread and wine up to the altar, where they are received and blessed in the eucharistic prayer, and given back to us in communion. Finally we are sent out in the company of Christ with the blessing of God to do his work in the world.

This step by step picture may catch the imagination. It can be seen as a wider and simple picture of taking in the love of God in Christ, and responding to it by putting ourselves in his hands, and receiving the risen strength of Christ through his sacrifice. This can stir a person or a whole congregation to find in the eucharist the great point of renewal in the week. A congregation will only do this if the service is thoughtfully and well done. For many it will need underlining in various ways; it will need variety both from the seasons and to stir interest. The service can generate a strong corporate life which will be a powerful force both to draw people to Christ and also to sustain them. Most of all the service can convey to us the wonder and the mystery of God's dealing with us.

*   *   *   *   *

Can we possibly find a way to meet all those requirements? The tendency is to say 'not in our little church, or with our limited resources'. There are however, many more avenues to be explored than most realise, and even more use to be made of limitations. One part of the answer is to see that you don't need to do everything the same way in all places, or all the time. There are many ways of doing each part of the service for us to explore. Christians have celebrated communion in many different

55

places from upper rooms and catacombs to large cathedrals, from the open air to hospital bedsides. Situations will limit the possibilities for such things as music and movement, colour and clothing, and even length and extent of prayer: the Alternative Service Book provides a shortened eucharistic prayer for a celebration for the sick. The size and shape of church buildings will make limitations. These have to be respected and worked with, and certainly work is required, but with it, it is possible to find all sorts of ways of making the point to parts of the service by using different parts of the church. This is one of the simplest ways of helping people both to see the different sections of the service, to sense the movement, and to find themselves being involved. The preparation and ministry of the word can be very simply conducted from a prayer desk, lectern and pulpit, with the intercessions taken from the centre of the nave. This brings the service among the people and makes a link with other services such as evensong. At the offertory the priest can move up to the sanctuary to carry the attention and interest of the people on to a further stage of the service. The congregation may go up to a sanctuary rail for communion, or if the space there is too small, communion can be given either from a rail in front of the nave, or with people coming to receive standing from the minister and assistant in front of the nave. Some may have room to move altars forward to the front of the nave, but others need not be anxious if they cannot do so, or try to force an altar into too small a space. A movement up to the sanctuary at the offertory can underline the action of the thanksgiving and communion, and the withdrawal at the end of the service can be made more expressive, if clergy leave the sanctuary immediately after the blessing, for their exit, turning as they reach it to give the final greeting from the west end. Even if there is no vestry at that point a space can be made for unvesting and leave the clergy ready to greet the congregation at the door.

The bringing of the bread and wine and the alms up from the nave by members of the congregation is a well-tried and familiar piece of action to many. This has gone on long enough to rebut the criticism that this practice implies that our offerings enable God's action, but it does make an opportunity for participation. It gives people the chance to think more deeply of the gifts of God to us, and of our response to him. The offertory sentences provide for all to say and express, 'Yours Lord is the greatness, the power, the glory . . . All things come from you and of your own do we give you'. The use of servers is not just a way of adding to sanctuary parties, or just of giving boys and girls a definite piece of work to do, though this is an important aspect; it provides an opportunity for representatives of the congregation to be further involved in the action and the movement of the service. It is worth taking pains to make sure that such people learn to move gracefully and purposefully, and care needs to be taken that their movements are designed to make this possible. Servers and their movements look much better if they are clothed in a full-length alb rather than the shortened surplice.

It is partly from this aesthetic angle that this question of the dress of ministers has to be judged; this is a valuable element of tradition, or the continuity of the life of the Church. The full length white alb was the undergarment of the later Roman Empire, and the short cloak or chasuble the indoor garment. When the Barbarians brought in trousers the Church kept the old garments; they were the garments of the Church of the martyrs. As the Church, particularly the monastic orders, spread across into the colder climates of northern Europe, the long alb was cut looser and shorter to make way for a fur pelisse underneath during the long offices and became the surpelisse or surplice; then monastic hoods or hoods and scarves appeared over them. It is unfortunate that in the Middle Ages elaborated interpretations were placed on the eucharistic vestments connecting them with the sacrificial priests of the Old Testament, so repeating Christ's sacrifice. This brought their rejection by the Calvinistic part of the Reformation, though Lutherans continued to use them, and Anglicans oscillated. With the recovery of the eucharist as the centre of Christian worship, it has seemed sensible and natural to many to recover the particular dress for the particular act. Usefully too, there has been a return to longer, more graceful chasubles in place of those cut on the Italian model. For many, more important than shape is colour; a chasuble in the season's colour gives an immediate point for attention, as does the changing frontal of an altar. So too a fuller cloth thrown all over an altar is often more effective. Colour and line do not end with vestments or altars; the eye may begin there, but will travel outwards, and congregations will do well to train themselves to care about the appearance of their churches. There may be little they can do in the way of redecoration, but there is much they can do in the way of cleaning and keeping tidy and free of clutter.

*   *   *   *   *

Congregations are often most aware of their limitations in the way of music. In scattered areas it is often difficult to find someone to play an organ or piano. Here perhaps most of all work needs to be done to deal with limitations; it may be the work of moving a piano into the church, where a good pianist may be better than a bad organist. Further work certainly needs to be done, both to help organists across all the churches, and also to help supply needy areas. Another step needs to be taken to gather groups of singers; it is a great blessing when a church has an organist who can train both a choir and congregation to sing. Sometimes it will be a different person who does this, who must work with an organist or pianist. The singing of hymns is a major part of people's worship and one of the simplest ways of people participating and beginning to feel and express their faith. There is a need to help people to sing well, but also to help them to sing good words. There are now a number of modern collections; certainly discrimination needs to be used both in the use of the old collections and of the new ones. There is a theological responsibility on a priest to chose suitable hymns in conjunction with his organist, to fit different points in the service. All too frequently congregations sing at the end of a service 'O enter then his courts with praise', when they could have been better helped to start with those words. A hymn between the readings needs to be kept short, even by leaving out verses; a hymn with a collection in it needs to be of sufficient length.

Well chosen hymns at the beginning of the service, between the readings, at the offertory and after communion, can be a simple way of marking points in a service and giving movement to it; more can be done by singing the choral parts of the service. In the revised services, the sung parts have now internationally agreed English texts. Though it is early in their life to produce great music to them, a number of composers have been giving

attention to this. Many congregations in this country still sing
John Rutter's setting which was written specifically for the
Series III version, and many sing the later forms of Dearnley
and Wicks, and of Sheppard. There should be more interchange
between the churches on these versions; there are a considerable
number of popular settings which have been written in the
Roman Catholic Church, both in this country and America. A
number of leading contemporary composers have written
modern classical settings for the revised services, and also made
arrangements of some of the shorter masses of Haydn, Mozart,
and Schubert. Wisely the Alternative Service Book also makes
provision for those, who sing settings for services written to the
old text, to use that old text at the appropriate places.

The offering of music is not confined to congregations or
choirs singing hymns or parts of the service; there may be other
offerings, vocal or instrumental at other points, or most
obviously organ music during the time of communion, or
during the cleansing of the vessels following communion.
Sensitively done, this can be a most valuable contribution to the
service. So, of course, is the music played before and after a
service; this is often an opportunity to use instrumental players,
and these may be used during the time of communion or at
some point such as the offertory. Folk music can be used quite
effectively at these points. This is one of the ways in which
judicious variety can be provided. The majority of congregations
have a mixture of people, and need a judicious mixture of
classical and popular; the important point is to try to preserve a
good standard in both. In view of the relatively short span of
acts of worship and the mixture of people, it does mean that
most music should be fairly direct, but not obvious; often many
enthusiasts, both for classical and popular music, fail to gain the
attention and sympathy of congregations through too indirect
music. This certainly doesn't mean that music should be
exhausted at its first hearing; good music grows on hearing, but
it will need to command a hearing in order to grow. Many may
need introducing to good music either by such things as a
practice of hymns or settings for the service, or by written or
spoken interpretation of the music.

*   *   *   *   *

The readings play a central part in the ministry of the word, and in many ways set the tone of a service. They have, through long tradition, been the point at which a special note has been given to the service for that Sunday, and variety given by a series of readings round the Sundays of the year. As the Church's year has developed, and time has passed, certain confusions of orders have resulted so that, for instance, the epistles and gospels for Trinity in the Prayer Book version have come from an upset order. All the churches have been giving thought to the revision of the scheme of readings; the Roman Church has produced a three-year lectionary; the joint Liturgical Group produced a new set on which most of the other churches have worked, which is partly in a one-year form and partly in a two-year form. The Anglican revised Lectionary for Sundays is adapted from this. It provides linked readings from the Old Testament, an epistle and gospel, around a theme for each Sunday. The Sunday material is strengthened now by the addition of a sentence to open the service for each Sunday, as well as one to introduce the 'after communion' section. These moves are a great encouragement to preaching from the theme on Sundays; all this can help a sense of the event of Sunday morning, to give a sense of expectancy, and later a way of reflection, to draw out the fruit for the week.

Attention to the readings can be assisted by care in the place and person involved in the reading; audibility is clearly the main test of both the place and person, and also visibility. Much can be gained by having a change of voices for the readings; traditionally reading the gospel was one of the specific functions of deacons, and other readings of those in minor orders. Certainly when a church is served by a number of clergy, the obvious way of using them is in the readings and the administration of communion. But the single-handed priest has the help of lay people to turn to; that help will need encouragement, and may need hearing first. It goes without saying that reading needs preparation; clergy can often learn from lay people in their care and preparation. There is much to be gained from having the contrast of male and female voices in two or more readings. The same result can be seen effectively by the occasional use of a group of readers with contrasting voices breaking up parts of the reading. This clearly needs preparation and rehearsal, but will often make a considerable impact. A further impact from time to time can be made by presenting a gospel or Old Testament reading in simple drama. This again needs careful preparation not least in the matter of visibility and audibility. A simple alternative is provided by a mime with the reading of the lesson in question.

Another variety of presentation of the readings is provided by liturgical dance. Congregations have been chary of this through its association with frenzy and nature worship. At the present time it is perhaps best presented by small specialist groups, some of whom now will produce a dance accompaniment to a whole eucharist. The development of dance in schools, however, offers the opportunity for many young people to use dance imaginatively and creatively. This can often lead itself to presenting a dramatisation of the readings in the ministry of the word. Such an interpretation may provide a new dimension to a service.

One last form of the presentation of the word may involve the movement of the congregation, rather than of dancers, in viewing an exhibition of art. A display of art in a church may arise from the offering of a particular group of artists, or through some group activity on the part of older or younger members of the congregation. These may form a striking interpretation of Christian faith, and in churches where there has been adequate room for display and movement, congregations have been encouraged to spend ten minutes or so looking at the pictures in the place of a sermon. This requires careful preparation to secure easy and quiet movement, but also sufficient interpretation and stimulus to thought. This can be helped by a brief introductory word, or by a commentary posted by the paintings.

* * * * *

An important part of the ministry of the word belongs to the sermon. Here the word is to become particular for this congregation at this moment. The congregation should feel a sense of shared responsibility with the preacher. They can do this by an expectancy beforehand, backed by prayer and response afterwards, both in deeds and words. Words are better if constructive; they can be extended to an on-going discussion group which can pass thoughts backwards and forwards with the preacher. The new Lectionaries emphasise the particularity of the Sunday by the correlation of the readings and the sentences, and so strengthen the case for preaching from the theme of the Sunday and its readings on most occasions. Even with a given theme, the three, or maybe two, readings will give considerable width of material; the very nature of the material, which has proved itself so long over history, provides continually new facets to those who are studying them closely. On the other hand, a priest or pastor who is closely concerned for the needs either of his flock or his neighbourhood, may find that he wants to take up some other aspects of Christian faith to make his particular point for this week, and this is fair enough if he makes clear the link he is making. Any preacher will need to make that link with his people, and may find that in any case it is better to make that link at the beginning of the sermon, and then to draw in the scriptures as he goes along, rather than produce a text at the beginning which often forms a blanket between himself and his hearers. There will be other times when preachers will want to have courses of sermons for their people at their main act of worship. Sometimes this can be done from the Creed or from the structure of the service, or from a season such as Lent or Advent. There may be need locally for other courses, but the themes in the new lectionary do themselves provide material for many courses. In any case it is useful to pick up links with the scriptures and certainly to link such sermons to the action of the eucharist.

Any Christian preacher needs to make sure that his sermon contains some element of the gospel, even though he feels he must address some subject, either topical or it may be ecclesiastical. There is no point in preaching a Christian sermon about it unless it contains some element of the good news of Jesus. Some sermons indeed are more concerned with the bad news; they need to balance criticism and denunciation with the note of trust and assurance derived from Christ. Any sermon needs to take off from the surroundings and concerns of the hearers. Though this may sometimes lead to an almost immediate reference to some point from the Bible or theology, more often this reference will come more gradually. It is certainly important that that reference comes and that there is a real working out of how it applies – but any application must come back to the lives and circumstances of the hearers. The sermon in the eucharist can often point to that intersection of God's action and life in the sacrament.

How long does it take to do all this in a sermon? It need not take too long; ten to fifteen minutes should be time enough. There may be occasions when the fulness of the content needs expanding for a minute or two more, but no more. This is not the place or time for the expansive lecture. This must be the ministry of the word in its context, looking forward to the sacrament; the overall pattern and pace of the service matters a good deal. The points will be all the better made if they are made with a careful clarity and brevity. This is not a limitation on preaching; it is a useful sharpening of it. Lay people can do much to assist that sharpening by showing their appreciation of clarity and brevity and by the questions they ask their preacher afterwards.

*   *   *   *   *

The immediate response to the ministry of the word comes in the declaration of faith in the Creed, and in the intercessions. These are both opportunities for participation, the return to the original 'we believe' form of the Nicene Creed reminds us that this is a corporate faith we express. We both contribute our own, but also can receive from faith of others. People feel the need for both of these at different times. The intercessions, spelt out in sections with responses, give to many people one of the best opportunities in the service to feel that they are really sharing in the prayer. This can be further extended by sharing the biddings in different sections. When people are sitting quite close together it is possible for people in their own places to do this. In a large congregation this is difficult to arrange, but it may be quite possible to arrange for two voices to alternate, or three each doing two, or it may be just one lay person doing the biddings. Much of the sharing must be done in the careful preparation of biddings – these need to be kept short, otherwise the intercessions easily become overloaded. In a small gathering it is quite possible for people to make spontaneous contributions, but this becomes more difficult on a large scale, and is easily monopolised by a few.

A further opportunity of participation is in the active giving of the peace by handshakes or embraces. This is a simple matter in a small gathering, or one gathered for a specific occasion. Here the action can be passed from one to the other and vary in form according to choice. In a larger gathering it will be more manageable for the action to be simple, by handshake, and passed by ministers to the congregation nearest to them, and then for everybody to exchange as they wish. In a large gathering too it must be remembered that some people's way of participation will be the receptive form, so it may be wiser there not to impose an active peace on every occasion, but to keep it for special ones.

More important than words or action in participation is the way in which the congregation can help people to feel they belong by respecting their invidiuality and maybe their reserve. The greeting at the beginning of the service draws people together to begin an act of worship. It will need to be preceded by a genuine welcome and concern for people as they arrive at a church. This need not be effusive, and may be largely done by a smile and the general indication of seats, and the provision of books. It will need further concern at the end of the service, often with some expression of interest and if possible with the offer of coffee or breakfast to follow. The parish breakfast was an important part of the parish communion movement. As the movement has widened there has been a tendency to move services to the 10 o'clock rather than 9 o'clock region, and to change the refreshment to follow to coffee. This is a very valuable occasion for a congregation to realise itself; it is well worth doing at the back of the church if there are no other premises available, but particular care needs to be taken to make sure it is not just for the regulars to greet each other. There needs to be a real open-eyed caring for all, both for the stranger and the infrequent, and also a respect for people at their different stages.

Another factor in fostering the community life of the congregation is through notices. Care needs to be taken that these do not clutter the service; much can be done by a notice on a wall or table, or by hand-outs, but these things may be too impersonal. Most congregations appreciate an expression of personal care and concern by notices; there is much to be said for these being given out at the beginning of services and being kept short. After the creed and immediately before the inter- cessions is another possible place. The third suggestion in the ASB, of before the final blessing is unfortunate and shows a lack of appreciation of the sacrament and the feeling of that moment.

*   *   *   *   *

One of the most important elements in the corporate sense of the congregation is the care it provides for children. It is very important to help young families to worship together. Children need the opportunity to grow into the life of the Church by participation. They are quick to appreciate the dramatic action of the eucharist, which has a much more direct appeal to them than mattins or made-up services. Wise congregations have learned that the eucharist is the service for the family. They have also learned over the years that it is better not to send children out after the first part of the service, for fear that communion is above and beyond them. They have now realised it is better to give children the alternative ministry of the word for their own understanding and participation in the first part of the service, and then to bring them in to help to share in the movement of communion and to appreciate in their own way something of the mystery of the sacrament. There has been welcome growth of the provision of Sunday Schools and crèches for children during the first part of the eucharist. Where premises allow, children should go straight to their own area to begin with, or else they can go out there during the opening hymn or canticle. The Sunday School can provide a parallel ministry of the word both for children and for the teachers, who certainly should be helped to appreciate this. There are courses of lessons now available geared round the new sets of readings to help this very thing. It will be a great assistance to parents to have children under five cared for in a crèche during the first part of the service. This can simply be arranged by rota of the parents involved, and some single friends; it will only need two or three adults to look after the children. These adults can be encouraged to look up for themselves and read the epistle and gospel beforehand with the provision of a simple note. They may pass something of this on by means of picture books amongst the toys of the crèche, and simple talking with the children.

The crux is the provision of rooms, which may be unobtainable in the case of the isolated country church. Yet there is often some vestry space which is vacated during the actual service, which can provided a retreat for the young children, maybe a belfry for the older children, or there may be a handy house near to the church to which a quick exit can be made. If a church is not blessed with adjacent rooms, it may be worth some considering a simple partition or thick curtain in a corner of the church to provide such a room; it may be simply gathering children in a back corner to work on their own with whispered instruction, which can add to the excitement, as I have seen myself. In cases where there is difficulty in finding any such provision, or where a congregation is only just beginning to appreciate the need to provide for families, useful advice for parents with young children is to come late and go early. A further help is to take them for a short walk during the sermon. This is not discourteous to the Lord, or to the clergy; it requires real thought and offering. The week's reading can be studied at home, and can provide an encouragement to pray on the way in and on the way out, and more particularly to get a sense of being part of the whole, in which the prayers will sustain us.

A further question arises with children at the other end of the age range; those who have gone up to the altar regularly to receive a blessing when their parents receive communion, will be impatient to receive communion at any rate from the age of 8 or 9 onwards. In the Church of England the debate on the age for confirmation has been going on for some decades. There has been value in the western practice of delaying confirmation until the age of understanding. Yet the growth of understanding must go on all through life. Once it seemed fair to delay to the senior school age of 11 or 12. In present day society the period between 12 and 15 often contains the most difficult years of adolescence; confirmation either side of this period seems to be preferable to

that within. The Anglican debate about initiation in the mid
70's, rejected admission to communion before confirmation,
but asked the bishops to confirm at an earlier age, when
suitable; in a churchgoing family 10 or 11 may be a more
suitable age. There has also been a welcome increase in the
number of adult candidates. The question is now under debate
again.

*   *   *   *   *

The attendance of whole families at the eucharist brings back to
people's minds the question of the sense of mystery and to
maintain it in the presence of small children. The task for all is
to explore further the Christian mystery, which centres in the
Word made flesh and the child of Bethlehem. It is noticeable
how Jesus used children as an example in the gospel. The
Christian mystery must combine both mystery and intimacy. As
Psalm 113 puts it, 'Who is like unto the Lord our God, that has
his dwelling so high; and yet humbleth himself to behold the
things that are in heaven and earth?' In the bread and wine we
receive Christ our Lord. As we receive him in our mixed
company of rich and poor, young and old, mothers with babies
in their arms, we are united in the body of this same Christ.
There is a mystery and a transcendence to be discovered in the
mixture of company. The naturalness of children and of
parents, if they are allowed to be relaxed, can help us to recover
some naturalness in our prayers, in the uninterrupted sweep of
prayer and music, and also amid the ongoing of life of the
family of God around us. If a congregation can see the
importance of this sharing in the wonder for the whole family of
God, and all the members of the family, it will help people to
relax, so that any undercurrent from children is a cheerful one
and not a strain and a pain. Much depends on the sense of
mutual care and awareness and indeed expectancy in a congregation. This will also lead to the adolescent and adult members
wanting to explore their faith further, and the shape and
language of the revised service will help them to enter more fully
into the great acts of God.

Expectancy, imagination, movement, wonder, are the gifts

that ordered worship can bring to people. They will be called out at different stages of the service. Expectancy can change the process of getting ready for a service from a general rush round by choir and congregation, to a purposeful seeing that everything is ready. This is particularly important where the priest has to serve, as often in the country, two or three churches, and move quickly from one to the other. There will be a task of preparation for both young and old to see that everything is ready for him when he arrives. This sense of expectancy can pass to the worshipper arriving, whether he or she comes leisurely or in a hurry, whether alone or coping with children. All can catch something of the great act of the week. Those who can come in good time will use some of that time in praying; the prayer needs to be a generous prayer, not merely for self but for others, both for those who can come to church and those who can not, ineed for the whole world and its need. That prayer can help to create an atmosphere in which people can come into a service quite happily late, if need be. The same sense of expectation can arise again at the sermon, both on the part of the congregation and the preacher. The same should be true of the intercessions, both on the part of those leading them and those sharing by response.

The movement of the service from the ministry of the word through the prayers, on to the peace, into the thanksgiving, should lead to a growing sense of wonder and expectancy. The sections of the thanksgiving have been divided by acclamation. Here the congregation should be spiritually on tip-toe. The phrase in the Lord's Prayer 'Your kingdom come, your will be done' can help the wonder of coming to communion. The open hand to receive the sacrament is an expression of expectation. The time after communion is for many a wonderful opportunity to pray. Many will be helped to do this if the ablutions follow, perhaps accompanied by quiet organ music, or singing by a choir. Some will be happy kneeling, but others will find it easier to sit and reflect; others in fact will be helped through the singing of hymns at this point. The prayer before the blessing 'Send us out, in the power of your spirit', and the dismissal after it, can help the worshippers go out both with a sense of wonder in response to the expectations with which they came in, and also with a new sense of expectancy, meeting what is to come in the company of Christ, crucified and risen. The journey will certainly have been worth it; those who have been open will have a new view and a new strength to go on with life's journey.

8

FINDING OURSELVES

Finding our way through the eucharist involves seeing something of both its shape and its movement. It is not difficult to see that we are involved in a great drama; it doesn't take long to appreciate that great drama is not just entertainment to pass away the time but is something which involves the beholder in sharing an experience. Great dramas, whether from the past of Shakespeare or the Greeks, or from the present, enrich experience, presenting to us a variety of facets. The eucharist is not just another service to get through; it is a great act where we are not just beholders but also participants, in which we share something very rich which will convey different points to us at different times.

It is not surprising that from earliest times Christians did not just celebrate the resurrection of Christ annually, but weekly on the first day of the week, and as the letters of St. Paul show, celebrated this in the eucharist. They saw themselves renewing their life in the crucified and risen Christ, and being built up in his body to the praise and honour of the Father. Christians soon began to find the richness of the communion relationship with Christ in the eucharist; those three strands we noticed from the New Testament provided the main avenues of exploration. It is through these that we can find our way into the action, or rather find the way in which the action involves and finds you and me. The eucharist proves to be for many people the place where they begin to find some sense of meeting with the Lord, of being confronted by him, or catching hold of him. This may come in the simple act of receiving communion, or in the quiet of reflection afterwards. It may come through the quiet of prayer or through music, the two coming together at 'Lift up your hearts'; it may come at the end of the service or it may well come in the act of preparation. Certainly by the help of those three avenues in our preparation for communion we can open up an effective way for finding the Lord, or being found by him in the act.

*   *   *   *   *

The basic response to the presence and gift of Christ offered in communion must be one of wonder. The New Testament passages as we have seen, offer some avenues into understanding this communion with Christ crucified, risen, ascended. At various points we meet this wonder of the action of the transcendent God focused in the marvel of Christ giving himself in communion, this has led to a whole tradition of reverence in church buildings. It has been expressed in the building itself with the focus at the altar, and sometimes by soaring arches or subdued lighting through stained glass windows. The tradition of quiet in church buildings is all part of this response, and the traditional act of genuflecting, or dropping on one knee in the approach to the altar, originally copied from Imperial court practices, is another. At one stage the thought of making communion the first food of the day was another natural response. Though we now have more varied timetables and a greater need for sustenance, there is still much to be said for making sure there is a break of some time after food, for Christ is here to meet us in food.

Undifferentiated wonder is an ambivalent approach. We need to take thought about the wonder. There is the wonder of the generosity of God meeting us in Christ, meeting us in the act of communion, offering us renewal and sustenance. The psalms chart for us the Jews' deep understanding of thankfulness in response to the wonder of God, 'Praise the Lord, O my soul, and forget not all his benefits' (Psalm 103). When a Jew asked for a blessing on a meal he did so giving thanks to God for his blessing in the past, trusting that he would bless again. So when Jesus took bread he gave thanks for his blessing. So the

71

thanskgiving or the eucharist has from the start been perhaps the most familiar name for the celebration of communion. Thankfulness therefore, will provide our main way to explore the avenue of the wonder of God's gift to us in communion.

The New Testament practice of meeting for the eucharist on the first day of the week suggests our giving particular thanks for what God has given us over the past week. Though we shall have given some thanks each evening in our prayers and at intermittent times, we can take a deeper and wider look over a week. We can see both what God has given us in good happenings and circumstances, but also what he has enabled in us, and indeed what he has enabled in other people. We are often slow to see this last, but even slower to admit the growth in ourselves, that God has enabled some good in us. Sometimes we are too taken up with our own success to realise the help which he has given us, but more often we are so taken up with our disappointments that we do not stop and see how much he has given us, in spite of those disappointments. Deeper thanksgiving is a great help in restoring our balance and courage to face life. It enables us to realise something of his presence with us, and then to look round to see his presence and help through other people, and to look for more to come. Thanksgiving in preparation, and during the eucharist, will certainly widen our horizons; we begin to appreciate something of the wonder of Christ's gift and presence to us.

Taking some care with thanksgiving can help us on the way to responding to the wonder of Christ's gift and presence in communion; we must also take steps to enter into the wonder of his sacrifice and find our way to share in it realistically. It means we must see our need to be changed and take his forgiveness and help. The broken bread and the wine poured out clearly look forward to his life given to meet human wrong on the cross, and answered in resurrection. So receiving communion gives us a share in this answer to wrong, for ourselves and for the world. We must take up the share for ourselves, if we are to help in this answer to the world. We shall need to examine ourselves and see where we have been wrong and require forgiveness. We have to overcome our physical and mental laziness, and also our physical and mental fears; and above all not fear to take his help and that of others. The necessity for change involves changing ideas and ways; this will often require seeking further information and help. As we receive the body and blood of Christ, given in love and obedience and raised in trust, we are asking to have Christ's death and resurrection reproduced in us. It is a simple step to go on from thanking God for the past week to recognising where we have fallen short in the past week, what we must confess and renounce, to what we must die. From this we can look forward to see what the Lord wants us to do in the next week in communion with him. Communion calls both for a renewal in honesty about ourselves, but also in trust in Christ's action within us.

Thinking about our responsibility will make us think about what other people need in the world around us, and leads us to the third strand of communion. As Jesus calls us to share in his life 'given for you and for many', he links us with our fellow communicants, near and far, and calls us to share his concern for the whole world and its unity. He offers us that life through his creaturely gifts of bread and wine, so he asks us to think about our responsibility for the natural world too. We shall not find all the Lord has in store for us, respond fully to his finding of us, unless we have some care for other people, and indeed some care for the whole creation.

We may find it difficult to cope with thoughts of the whole world. It is wise to have some plan of praying for different parts of our lives and the people we touch on different days of the week; the gathering up of the week before communion gives an opportunity to think of whom and what we want to pray for specially in each Sunday eucharist. This part of preparation can help us to follow and take our share in the intercessions in the service under its different heatings. We can also have the sense of taking our concern to the altar and of going out with the assurance of communion with the risen Christ. This can help us considerably in our prayers for other people, and save us from nagging God with our worries; it can help us to share our concerns with him, and to know that he shares with us, whether our prayers are for physical healing, or for spiritual conversion, about the world or about our work. Our work is not too slight for us to offer the Lord in the bread and wine, which are themselves the product of human work; through them we receive the life of Christ who worked and suffered, and died and

73

rose, and he will go out with us to our work, and through our work, out to others.

We can, in the various series, join in saying or singing, just before the communion, a revised form of the Agnus Dei, 'Jesus, redeemer of the world, give us your peace'. Redemption is a slow and patient process – in both senses of patience, in suffering, and in waiting, as Paul made very clear in the eighth chapter of Romans, 'The created universe groans in all its parts as if in the pangs of childbirth', but he adds later, 'It is Christ – Christ who died and more than that was raised from the dead, who is at God's right hand and indeed pleads our cause'. Gradually and patchily we see something of that effectiveness of Christ, in the world, working in other people, or even in ourselves, if we give time to that deeper thanksgiving. So we are heartened to return to patient intercession.

Those simple steps of preparation – looking deeply over the week to thank God for what has been given around us, through other people, and in ourselves, taking the trouble to see where we have been wrong and where we need to change, and looking forward to where we can take new steps with Christ in the coming week, bringing to him in prayer our concerns for other people in need, the world and its causes, and something of our own work – these strands all hold together. We shall find they form an important gathering point in our week's prayers, and can open the way for us to catch vital moments of the eucharist; and though we may not have great feelings on the way through, we can come to realise at the end we have a real share in a great work of Christ, and he has that great share in us. It is worth taking steps to allow time, probably on Saturday, for this gathering up. For many people it may be better to do it earlier in the evening, before going out, and it may be a help to do it with some notes on a pencil and paper; we may have to deal with interruptions and with our own easy distractions. It is often in the taking of such practical steps that we first discover that somehow the Lord helps us along, and we begin to realise the Holy Spirit does work. So we discover, as we find our way into the wonder of communion by taking these practical steps, that the Lord finds his way into our lives week by week at very practical points. We begin to discover the truth of Coleridge's words, 'In short whatever finds me, bears witness for itself that it has proceeded from a Holy Spirit, even from the same Spirit, which remaining in itself, yet regenerated all other powers, and in all ages entering into holy souls, maketh them friends of God'.*

*   *   *   *   *

Festivals and Saints' days can play an important part in finding ourselves in relationship with Christ and the world as we go round the year. Christians of different traditions and at different stages of life find that the eucharist takes on a particular significance for them at the great Church festivals. Easter is the most obvious occasion; communion with the risen Christ gives us the truth of every Sunday. Easter communion has long been in many traditions the minimal requirement for continuing church membership, but there is much more in it than this. Following Christ through Holy Week can give a Christian his or her first glimpse of the significance of communion during the week, perhaps first on Maundy Thursday evening, as we remember the institution of the Last Supper. This can then lead on to the seeing that communion during the first days of the week is the simplest way to share with Christ in those days of the great week, day by day, Monday to Thursday. Some Reformed parts of the Church have seen a particular point of receiving communion on Good Friday, taking up Paul's thought of 'showing forth the Lord's death until he come'. The major tradition of the Church has been to abstain from communion on Good Friday and Easter Eve, as a way of measuring the real loss of Christ, and of seeing more clearly in contrast the wonder of communion with the risen Lord. The immediate preparation for Easter on Easter Eve was the traditional time for Christian baptism; the service was expanded with readings taking up the pilgrimage of the People of God from Exodus to the resurrection, and leading on to baptism and confirmation, and to communion at midnight or daybreak. This has passed after the first five centuries into the lighting of the paschal candle on Easter Eve and the renewal of baptismal

---

* Coleridge 'Confessions of an Enquiring Spirit' Letter 1 quoting Wisdom 27

vows. There has been a welcome return to see the excitement of Easter Eve, and using it as an occasion for adult baptism where possible, and otherwise for the renewal of baptismal vows. Some will end with a midnight communion, though many still prefer to wait for the light of Easter Day.

Christmas, with its message of the Word made flesh, has its penitential preparation of Advent. Nowadays, many carol services are brought forward from after Christmas to before Christmas to fit in with school and other arrangements. Their words however, can be turned to useful preparation. Most obviously Phillips Brooks' fine words at the end of 'O little town of Bethlehem' – 'cast out our sin and enter in, be born in us today . . . O come to us, abide with us, our Lord Emmanuel'. We need to work hard to make our time and preparation before Christmas. It can be quite simply done if trouble is taken, as when tying up a present. For many the excitement is increased by making communion right at the start of the day, in a midnight communion, and it is worth making sure we get some time of quiet in the hours before that. Many prefer to wait to Christmas morning. But the occasion is often one that can reawake the awareness of those who have been absent since last year, and timely help at a service with books or a judicious reference to some particular words of carols, can often help a new awareness.

Whitsun has lost its public holiday in this country but offers itself obviously for an occasion for Church and congregational celebration, as the birthday of the Church. Whitsun communion can give an opportunity for thinking about building up the body of Christ when we feed on his body and blood. Ascension Day has a still harder task, a weekday without a public holiday, but challenges Christians to celebrate the great feast of the Lord on a working day, either in the morning or in the evening, and so lends itself very much to thought about worship, which can be helped by the hymns and sermons. Ash Wednesday is another day which still catches the imagination of Christians to enter on the refresher course of Lent, again either with a celebration in the morning or in the evening. The weeks of Lent offer an obvious time when people may see the point of mid-week celebrations.

Saints' days are the other very obvious markers through the

year. The commemoration of the deaths of great Christians can be seen as in a sense their heavenly birthday parties. We can give thanks and gain stimulus when something is known of their lives, and at all times it gives a great sense of the company of Christian people across the ages. A saint's day may give a particular excitement to a weekday morning, or a natural occasion for a joyful celebration on a weekday evening, with a useful opportunity for the congregation during the week to gather afterwards for some particular part of its business or social life. The patronal saints of a parish should be a major occasion for celebration, as also would be All Saints' Day.

Michaelmas celebrates the angels, not the saints, but can open new vistas to people or new directions; they call to mind not just the great company of worship which extends not just across the Church, the faithful departed and the saints, but to the heavenly spheres; the 'Holy, holy, holy,' can take new meaning. At the same time the Bible sees angelic beings as pictures of the cosmic struggle, a struggle that extends across the universe and of which we are aware in many ways today – the forces that seem to go beyond individuals to the social and economic scene, and the natural order. It is for the redemption of all this that we share in the body and blood of Christ offered for us, and for the whole world.

* * * * *

Days of Holy Week and Lent and Saints' days have led many Christians to discover the excitement of communion on weekdays. For some congregations, especially in the country this will only be possible for special occasions and on the one mid-morning a week. In towns there is more opportunity. Some meet this by offering different times on different days of the week. Others have a more regular run of morning or evening times with one or two extras to suit various groups of people. Some will make their way there to find a particular help for some day's need; it may be new work, or an important decision, or someone's illness, or an occasion of happiness, or anniversary. Some may find it a simple step to make a regular practice on a regular day of the week. Preparation for weekday communion should be simpler than for a Sunday; it can be the normal elements of prayer, thanksgiving, penitence and looking forward, and prayer for others, with a particular thought of the communion of the morrow, both for ourselves and also in prayer for others. We do well to look forward the night before, whether the weekday celebration is in a morning or an evening. A parish church, if it is wise, will have a list of intentions for prayer for every day of the week to be used both in the corporate worship of the church in daily celebrations, and also at home for private prayer.

Worshipping on a weekday underlines the relationship of the eucharist to the working world. There is help for that world in the very action of the service; the offering of the bread and wine in response to the command of Christ is an offering of the products and raw materials of our world, not as an act of generosity on our part, but as a response of thankfulness, and recognition of how much we owe to him for our life, and what we owe in service to him. The relating of this to his death and resurrection in the thanksgiving prayer will remind us that he knows and faces all the difficulty of the working world, and the reception of the sacrament will remind us that we share the fruits of his risen life and go out with him to that work. The eucharist can be shared in a group who want to undertake some work together. They may well help their action by carrying their planning further after a weekday evening communion; sometimes this can lead to some immediate action such as visiting or undertaking some piece of service. Such specific connections can then help to promote the wider thought of prayer and communion leading to action. Action conceived in this way will always be conscious of its incompleteness; we shall see there is much more to be done; and this will ask for concerns to be brought back in intercession and intention to communion, so that a whole continuous cycle of prayer and action is set up.

*   *   *   *   *

Communion with the crucified and risen Christ has obvious relevance to the making of new beginnings. In this country this is shown most dramatically in the Coronation Service, which is, in fact, a communion service with the communion coming as the final act when the Sovereign, having been given all the symbols of state, receives the sacrament which can turn the symbols into reality. Not surprisingly the great moments of ordination of Christian ministers, deacons, priests and bishops, takes place in the same setting of communion. It is good too that increasingly now the act of confirmation, seen as the completion of baptism and the beginning of the adult life as Christians, takes place in the contect of communion.

We can take the cue from these to see the help that communion can be for the humbler beginnings of a new job or some new undertaking, or an examination. We can both bring our own offering of preparation and intention to the altar at such a time, and also our need of help and of deepening of trust. In the same way we can bring our thanksgivings; it is sensible to return to the altar to give thanks after success in examination or the completion of a piece of work, or the celebration of a time or anniversary. Many of the occasions in church or state, such as confirmation, ordinations, or coronations, have this double aspect of thanksgiving and celebration on one hand, and prayer and offering on the other. We are often stronger on praying than on thanksgiving, and we do well to look for the occasions to bring our thanksgiving to the eucharist. Birthdays and wedding anniversaries are obvious occasions; there are other private thanksgivings to mark, and group ones when a communion can give a deeper dimension to a celebration.

Marriage is both one of the great thresholds of life, and also one of the great celebrations. It calls for commitment in the promises 'till death us do part', and calls out the hope that love and joy may last. Communion gives us the pledge of the possibility. Popular songs about marriage speak of leading to the altar, but we often forget that this is for communion, the promises having taken place as a step on the way, as in a sense an offertory in the eucharist. The Alternative Service Book explains this in the appendix of the service; it is not indicated in the main text, and so runs the danger of being overlooked both by couples and clergy. If they look at it seriously they will see that this fulfils the understanding of Christian marriage, explains the movement of the service, and gives body to it. It is quite simply done, following the preface and actual marriage by the signing of the register, and then proceeding to the altar rail for collect, epistle, and gospel, and address – then straight to the Peace, giving an opportunity for the bride and bridegroom to kiss each other, and then on to the Thanksgiving Prayer. A special preface is provided 'now we give you thanks because you have made the union between Christ and his Church a pattern for marriage between husband and wife'. As the couple receive communion, so they have the opportunity to see that their marriage and their lives together is part of Christ's whole redemptive work in putting the world together in sacrifice and love. As the marriage service concentrates on the couple, the traditional practice of the couple communicating alone is quite fitting, and has the advantage of not dividing the congregation into those who are communicants and those who are not. With suitable use of music it is quite possible to get through the service in this form in 45 minutes.

*   *   *   *   *

Often we are most conscious of our need for help in our low moments; many admit that their obvious times of prayer are in sickness or troubles, and come to look back on these rather nostalgically. They forget that trouble and sickness also create difficulties for them in praying. They are right, however, to see that these can be openings into prayer and it is well worth thinking of ways through the accompanying difficulties. This is particularly true in sickness; the fact that Jesus gave us communion out of his suffering, and the disciples took up this help in the light of the resurrection, offers a particular link for our prayer and help in sickness. Often people say they don't feel up to it, or 'I want to feel my best', forgetting that God finds us and offers us his help at our worst moments. One of the pieces of the Church's work which has received most attention is its ministry to the sick. This has resulted in the provision of chaplains of all the main traditions of church life in this country – Anglican, Roman, and Free Church, to all the National Health hospitals in the country. Quite a number of patients, in the modern quick turnover, will not be conscious of this, but he or she has only to ask and a chaplain can be alerted and communion will be available. This is equally true of those who are at home; all the country is covered by parishes or territorial structures of the churches. Again in the large numbers of population and the decreasing number of clergy, people may not be always aware, but they have only to ask. Clergy know that from their ordination they have sometimes to be stirred to respond to it.

In most hospitals, and in most home situations, communion for the sick will be brought from elements consecrated in church. This will be kept in an aumbry or safe specially reserved for the purpose, or it may come direct from a service. It will often come in the form of intinction, with wine dropped on a wafer, for obvious safety in transport. The giving of communion will be quite brief – the collects for purity and for the day, the general confession and absolution, maybe a reading from the gospel, a brief moment of intercession, the prayer of humble access and the giving of communion – and a moment of thanksgiving. For most patients in bed this is quite enough, and it may well be reduced. In any case they can have the knowledge of the worship with the church around them in which they are sharing. In some cases there will be company with patients put together in a ward, or at home with neighbours coming in to share communion with the sick or housebound. Sometimes in such a home situation or in an isolated hospital it may be simplest to celebrate communion briefly at the bedside or the ward, for which the new prayer book provides a shortened thanksgiving prayer. For many communion in sickness, as on holiday, can be the opportunity to find new depth, to find God anew and to find concern for others' needs. So too for others, praying for the sick, particularly for friends, may be an opportunity to enter more deeply into the intercession and intention in communion. Most churches will keep lists of those to be remembered in the intercessions.

If the sacrament given in the night Jesus was betrayed speaks closely to the sick, it speaks even more clearly about death and bereavement. As we receive communion with Christ in his death and resurrection, we can see that he understands and stands by us in death; it is the pledge of sharing his life which offers us solid hope of life beyond death. The prayers, and above all the actual words of communion speak of the body and blood of

Christ keeping us in eternal life. It is a natural thought to try to administer communion to people in the closing moments of their life; it can be a simple focus of assurance to them and to those watching, when this is possible. For various reasons it may not be possible, but the knowledge of a communicant life beforehand will be strong assurance. The sacrament will also be a clear focus for prayer for the departed and for our sense of fellowship in the communion of saints. The increasing individualism and sense of fear in the Middle Ages brought excessive concentration on purgation which produced the chantry masses for the dead. At the Reformation there was an unfortunate reaction away from all thought of prayer for the dead. One of the odd good fruits of world wars was to bring many Christians back to prayer for their departed friends.

* * * * *

There are considerable helps and riches for us to explore in communion with Christ, as he sustains us with his body and blood at moments great and small, as our life unfolds stage by stage. That gathering up the week in preparation for Sunday communion is a vital stage of that unfolding, and we begin to see that life as sharing with Christ, and not as one week after another. The great festivals marking the seasons of the year can take us further; beneath the terms imposed by educational bodies, lies the fact that the life of individuals runs in terms. The Church's year gives an opportunity to stop and appreciate this pattern, which like that of nature is a call to growth. Christmas, Easter, and perhaps autumn festivals such as Michaelmas, with its pictures of the struggles of good and evil, call us to look back in deeper thanksgiving, and also to look within in self-examination and repentance. These are obvious occasions to claim what the Prayer Book calls the benefit of absolution both in spoken confession and forgiveness. So we can look forward in communion with Christ to a new stage. So the years can take us forward with the marking of marriages and anniversaries, and other high points, and the sustaining of sickness, so that we can see that life itself and death can be part of growth with Christ. We can appreciate the care that finds us in Christ every time the sacrament is adminstered to us with those words 'may the body and blood of Christ keep you in eternal life'. So we can pray with assurance 'your kingdom come, your will be done on earth as in heaven'.

9

FINDING RENEWAL, UNITY AND MISSION

Does communion really make a difference to life? Many who ask this question are content with too limited an answer, asking does it make a difference to them subjectively – 'will it help me?' There is a much wider question, which often haunts people without their having the courage to turn and face it; does our Christian worship really affect the world, and the whole structure of life? It may seem almost too hopeful to ask it, but it is not. We have seen that the help for ourselves is not to be reduced to a subjective reminder of the passion of Christ, as Christians at certain times have done; it is the objective gift of God, relating us to the whole work of Christ in his life, death and resurrection. That objectivity and that work can help us begin to see that this is saying and doing something to the whole of life, and not just to us.

The effectiveness and the objectivity of God's action in the eucharist stem from the Last Supper, and the events of the following days. Christ's words and actions at the supper pointed forward to what was about to happen to him. What followed immediately happened through the intricate political actions and reactions of men and women, some in places of responsibility in Jewish society and of the Roman Empire, and of others in the mass of the crowd. Jesus gave himself to his Father in obedience, and to those around him in reconciling love, not in a vacuum or in a secluded place of prayer, but in the forum of parties and crowds and individuals, amid a typical cross-section of human society. We can now see how different groups in that society took up positions which produced a combination of forces to bring about the unjust condemnation and execution of Jesus, in a way that is all too familiar in our own world. The Sadducees found their own conventions threatened, and the Pharisees their own reforming zeal out-matched by the deeper demands of Jesus; the crowd found that Jesus disappointed their hopes of a Jewish revival, but the Roman authorities thought that he might be too dangerous. Add to these the individual reactions of a Pilate and a Peter and a Judas. Jesus faced the basic human reactions of fear and pride; he dealt with the realities of human psychology. We can watch him dealing with different types from Judas with his words, 'would you betray the Son of Man with a kiss?', to the soldier, 'Father, forgive them they know not what they are doing'. That taking of the hammer blows is a pointed illustration of his reconciling love which takes in the evil and will not force a reply; he will wait for the reply which comes from the other side of death, from his Father. That answer makes possible the forgiveness and the renewal of his followers, and the spread of their newfound faith. That faith spread against the realities of the opposition of a totalitarian empire; it did so through his followers' sense of sharing in the passion of its Lord. He gave them the pledge of this sharing in the broken bread and poured out wine 'on the night he was betrayed'. They found they were offered communion with Christ, who is effective in the real world of human society, and the pressures of parties, and of human actions and reactions.

*   *   *   *   *

Jesus saw communion as the means of handing on his life in the night in which he was betrayed. Significantly he gave it to us in bread and wine, in terms of human feeding, in its aspects both of necessity and of celebration. Food brings us both the fruits of creation and the results of human labour upon those fruits. Jesus lived his life in the ordinary everyday relations of buying and selling, eating and drinking; in this act he makes contact with us in our everyday life of buying and selling, eating and drinking, and the vast fabric which that involves. The fruits of the earth and the labours of men cause us much anxiety, perhaps in the reverse order.

Certainly the fabric of our life is much more complicated than that at the time of Jesus, but basic needs remain the same. The simplicity of the act of communion in bread and wine may be useful to bring us back to basic needs. Feeding is an important indicator of the degree of our concern about our standards of living; many western Christians will admit that they are probably too concerned about this, and probably eat too much. The fact that Jesus meets us in this way may help us to take feeding seriously, both our own consumption and the hunger of others; as the Lord shares his life with us both, we are called to share our plenty with the hungry. At the same time Jesus invites us to an act of celebration, and the wine is a reminder of this aspect. Communion assures us that he would still have us rejoice, but we must combine this with a sense of responsibility about our use of the good world. This double thrust of communion assures us that Jesus meets us in all the intricacy of our business, whether it is directly concerned with food, either in the kitchen or the food industry, or indirectly, as nearly every form of business and service is.

The realisation that we share communion not only with those who kneel beside us in the church, and even across the country, but also with those across the world, reminds us that we must be responsible to them. We have rightly built up a concern in this country to ensure a basic standard of living for all. We have not yet learned that the increasing pressure to raise the standard of living is often done by one section of the community at the expense of another in this country; it is certainly done by this country at the expense of other parts of the world. Our sharing in communion should remind us that we must have that concern about basic standards of living for the whole human race, and not just the fortunate fifth in which we live, which at present takes four-fifths of the resources. 'We who are many are one body, for we all partake of one bread' (1 Cor. 10.17), provides us with a regular reminder of the needs of others. It also reminds us that this is the needy world in which Christ lived and gave himself to meet the selfishness of men and women, to help us to give. We can bring the needs of the world to him at the altar in his realism and effectiveness.

He gives himself to us in bread and wine, the fruit of men's labours on the fruits of nature. Many traditional liturgies and many recent revisions have begun their thanksgiving prayers at the centre of the eucharist with thanks to God for the work of creation and some have specified the gifts offered in the bread and wine. This thanksgiving is not to be confined just to the elements of that particular eucharist. We can thank and therefore trust God, for the whole of creation, and his whole provision for us. We need this thankfulness, and even more the trust arising from it, increasingly at this present time, as we face the problems in world hunger, and more searchingly the shortage of resources, behind the hunger. People often think first of the resource of oil, and only then go on to think of the deeper question of the resource of food. We begin to see that we must act responsibly about these resources of food and must right the wrong of a good deal of irresponsible use of resources. There is an irresponsible way of saying that science is bound to produce an answer, which is matched by an equally irresponsible attitude of saying that scientists will only make the matter worse. We need to be responsible and calm about the use both of science and redeemer. We need a thankfulness and a confidence in God both as creator and redeemer, and this is what Jesus offers in communion in bread and wine. He offers himself to us broken and poured out in answer to the selfishness and irresponsibility of human beings in the present physical world. He offers us this in the fruits of the earth, and gives us this pledge from which we go out to work with trust and unselfishness and responsibility to use those resources fairly and develop them with all the skills he gives us, and to share them for the good of all. But he gives us this from a focus which is entirely realistic about the opposition of human life and its obstinacy, if only we have the eye to see it. We need to look at the two-way sharing of life with Christ in communion.

On the one hand we can see that the Lord gives us the opportunity to go out from the communion renewed for the new week. It also covers the renewal of possibilities with the whole world, and we have seen this work through nations in the course of history. As the report from the Lima conference of the World Council of Churches, Faith and Order Commission said – 'The eucharist shows us that our behaviour is inconsistent in face of the reconciling presence of God in human history: we are placed under continual judgment by the persistance of unjust relationships of all kinds in our society, the manifold divisions on account of human pride, material interest and power politics and, above all, the obstinacy of unjustifiable confessional oppositions within the body of Christ'.†

*   *   *   *   *

It is fair enough to reply that if Christians are to be concerned for the renewal of society they must first have a concern for the renewal and the unity of the Church itself. It has often been said that the failure and division of the churches is the strongest argument against belief in God. That argument is quickly turned; the foolishness and obstinacy of man would have wrecked the Church long ago had these been the only factors in its life,. There are few stronger signs of the ceaseless activity of God the Spirit than the continued life of the Church, contradictory as it has often been, yet subject to continued revival and renewal. We can be thankful for all the work of renewal both in worship and other ways which has been going on over recent decades. We can be thankful too that we live in a time when old and new forms of worship go on side by side, so that we experience some of the tensions of renewal.

Those tensions were experienced back in Paul's time when the new wine of the gospel burst the old skin of Judaism. The new faith of Christians struggled with a variety of human experience and self-assertion: Paul had to bring his quarrelling Christians in Corinth to their senses; 'What I mean is this, each of you is saying 'I am Paul's man, or I am for Apollos, I follow Cephas or I am Christ's'; is Christ divided'? (1 Cor. 1.12). He was trying to get them to see how they had things out or proportion, and his clinching argument is 'When we break the bread, is it not a sharing in the Body of Christ? Because there is one loaf, we many as we are, are one body; for it is one loaf of which we all partake' (1 Cor. 10.17). It is not surprising that Christians have had to work their own unity out painfully in successive

---

† Baptist Eucharist and Ministry Geneva 1982 p. 14

generations. The test has always been to bring people back to communion one with another.

There were passing recoveries in the early Church; there was a near miss at recovering the split between East and West at the Council of Florence in the 15th century. There were attempts at it by both sides of the Reformation without success, and similarly at the Restoration in England in 1660. This present century has brought unions within the Church of Scotland and in Methodism, and the missionary conference at Edinburgh in 1910, which gave the impetus to the world ecumenical movement. Some unions between Free Churches in different parts of the world followed, but the significant move came with the formation of the Church of South India in 1947, bringing together for the first time episcopal and non-episcopal churches, and to be followed by union in North India and Pakistan in 1972. In the 1960's the Orthodox Church began to play its part in the World Council of Churches, and observers from the Church of Rome began to take an active part after the second Vatican Council.

The Church of England in this country has often claimed to hold together in one church the tradition of Catholic faith and order with the insights of the Reformation. When it comes to working this out in practice, it has tended to lose its nerve; it drew back from a plan for union with the Methodists in 1972, and it did so again after discussing the possibilities of a covenant of recognition of sacrament and ministries with the Methodists and the United Reformed Church ten years later. It looks over its shoulder at the possibility of sharing communion with the Roman Catholic Church encouraged by the agreed statement of the Anglo/Roman Catholic Commission, but still awaits any definite move.

Amidst these hesitancies and uncertainties, one thing is certain, that the call to express the unity offered to us by communion with Christ will not go away. It has already brought the churches closer, so that the argument often put in the past that shared communion must wait until a sharing of understanding and of ministries is reached by the Churches, no longer seems so forceful. We find we are at a stage of commitment to the search for unity which does call for sharing in communion; in 1971 in passing Canon B15 the General Synod of the Church of

England agreed to give communion to communicant members of other churches. The Free Churches have already practised this for some years; the Roman Catholics do not, though in many cases exceptions are made and invitations given. The Orthodox do not practise this, but allow for some latitude in practice and lay great stress on the value of experiencing each other's communion services. For many Christians this experience is made available once a year in the Week of Prayer for Christian Unity. The value of worshipping together can be simply extended to other times of the year by a local church inviting its neighbours of other traditions to attend the celebration of one of its particular occasions, such as a patronal festival or an anniversary.

In the meantime in the 1960's the discussions between the churches had taken a more positive turn. The Anglican/Roman consultations began from a preparatory commission in 1967, and led to the positive agreements that we have seen about memorial and sacrifice in 1970. The discussions of the Faith and Order Commission of the World Council of Churches turned at the Montreal conference in 1963 to looking towards policy consensus, instead of stating differences. In 1975 they set before the Church the task of achieving 'one Baptism, one Eucharist, and a mutually recognised Ministry', and this led to the notable document from the Lima conference in 1982, 'Baptism, Eucharist and Ministry' – a notable document as the commission includes Roman Catholics and Orthodox, as well as the rest of the spectrum of the World Council of Churches. At the time of writing the document is being considered by all the churches for an answer for the world Faith and Order Commission.

The Lima document makes a number of important points about the eucharist, as well as those already quoted – 'The eucharist opens up the vision of the divine rule which has been promised as the final renewal of creation, and is a foretaste of it. Signs of this renewal are present in the world wherever the grace of God is manifest and human beings work for justice, love and peace . . . Reconciled in the eucharist, the members of the body of Christ are called to be servants of reconciliation among men and women and witness to the joy of resurrection'. (page 14, para. 22).

The report adds telling practical points, 'Christian faith is deepened by the celebration of the Lord's Supper. Hence the eucharist should be celebrated frequently. Many differences of theology, liturgy and practice are connected with the varying frequency with which the Holy Communion is celebrated. As the eucharist celebrates the resurrection of Christ, it is appropriate that it should take place at least every Sunday'. (para. 16, page 30/31).

*   *   *   *   *

The Lima report makes very clear that this deepening of faith is not just an end in itself, or for the strengthening of the individuals for themselves; it is strengthening to help us to reach out. In another paragraph it says, 'The eucharistic community is nourished and strengthened for confessing by word and action the Lord Jesus Christ who gave his life for the salvation of the world. As it becomes one people, sharing the meal of the one Lord, the eucharistic assembly must be concerned for gathering also those who are at present beyond its visible limits, because Christ invited to his feast all for whom he died. Insofar as Christians cannot unite in full fellowship around the same table to eat the same loaf and drink from the same cup, their missionary witness is weakened at both the individual and the corporate levels'. (page 15, para. 26).

The readings in the ministry of the word in the first part of the communion service should remind us of this call to reach out. By their very nature the epistles and gospels in the New Testament bring us to the source of the Church in mission. Those letters of Paul began the Christian writing as a means of communication with those small groups of Christians gathered round the Roman Empire. It was from the telling of the things of Jesus in these groups that the gospels were put together to extend the mission of these small groups. We need to be reminded of this again and again. A preacher can usefully refer to this as he makes the link between the gospel and epistle addressed to the group of Christians in the first century, and its message on a particular Sunday to the group of Christians in front of him. This is good news indeed for small congregations in the country or in a city church; they can still be Christ's mustard seed, or his leaven, as were Paul's congregations in Galatia or Corinth; larger congregations need reminding of the ninety per cent who are still outside. All can be helped by the New Testament to recover that hope which took the gospel across the world against the growing of a totalitarian power. It is possible to spread the good news, whether it has to be done against indifference or embarrassment, or under active persecution; we are not asked to do this in our own strength, but in communion with Christ and his dying and rising life.

Those first communities of the Church round the Mediterranean seem to have spread the gospel by a combination of outside discussion and the faithfulness of the groups in meeting for the breaking of the bread. Certainly it was these meetings for worship which the persecution of the Empire did its best to stop. Christians in this century perhaps have thought too little about this major means of helping spread the gospel by bringing people to see something of the heart of Christian worship in the eucharist; communion is the simplest visual aid in which those enquiring into the faith will see something happening. They begin to see the possibility of a sense of participation and real meeting with Christ; often they will begin to experience something of the mystery of the communion of heaven and earth. Any church needs to be aware that there are likely to be one or two such people present even when least expected; clergy can help them, with quiet but clear directions; coffee afterwards can be an opportunity to meet such people. There needs also to be a readiness to recognise that some people want to slip into church and slip out. Bringing others to share in the experience of worship will be part of a long and wide process. The process will go through ups and downs; there will be long periods with nothing explicitly said, but it will be important that at some juncture we are able to say something to help interpret life, and to open up the vision of life in response to God in company with Christ.

In all this process it is important that the faith is not a self-conscious faith, it must be a more God or Christ-conscious faith. We need to understand for ourselves and to help others to understand, that faith is not something we do, but trusting in God's action in Christ, and making room for that action in us. That faith is exemplified very well in our openness to receive his life in the open hand stretched out in communion, and furthermore in the pattern of being ready to die for ourselves and rise to a new life with him week by week. This faith will be tested in the ups and downs of the long process of befriending and praying for others, and very much needs sustaining and bringing back again to Christ, in communion. This will enable us to see that the task of sharing faith is not ours to do by ourselves; it is the work of Christ that he shares with us. When we have such a resource, in time it becomes apparent to people; the invitation to share the experience of worship need not wait until the end of the process, but can often come in much earlier than we expect.

*   *   *   *   *

It is a mistake to think that if we recommend the Christian faith to enough people all would be done to effect the union of the Church, or the righting of the world. It is also a mistake to think that if we could only effect the reconciliation in society, that all would be well, or for that matter that if we could only express the unity of the Church all would be well. We have to work away at all three together, but we can't do any of these things in a vacuum. We have to work away at these amid the strong forces of our society. We do well to take note of two sets of forces which are in many ways contradictory to one another, so that people tend to only see one and forget the other. Many people are aware that there is a strong force of secularism. The Bible itself shows the concern of God for his created order, reinforced by the incarnate life of Christ. It also shows the freedom God has given the world and man. It is all to the good that we have developed an understanding of human autonomy; yet it is clear that a view of the autonomy of the world has grown to excessive proportions, even to regarding the universe as a closed system. This view leads back to the suppression of human freedom, and on a large scale to a totalitarian state, as the communist world has shown. Long before that, materialism leads to great conflict of interests; these may start in the struggle for freedom and justice, but they soon become struggles for differentials, advantages, and on to power and privileges. It is no accident there has been an increasing polarisation both in this and other western democracies, but also in countries behind the Iron Curtain. This is the field of the self-contradictory forces of materialism.

It is no accident or irrelevancy that Jesus met his death at the hands of a totalitarian empire, and in a local society which had often perverted its religious tradition for materialistic ends, and where opposing parties combined to oppose him with violence. He met those forces and that violence with complete self-giving and trust in his Father, which was answered in that resurrection life which he shares with us in communion, to help us to meet the polarised forces of materialism which impinge on us. We do not have to retreat from the world to pray and worship; he enables us to walk upright into the wind of the world's disorder in company with Christ, and take hold of his redemptive life and work.

In fact we need to take heed of the other, and more subtle, forces which tend to catch us in a cross wind; they are more difficult to place. They might be described under the name of a post-Christian society, or of conventional religion. As with the other forces, these have much good in their origin. We have inherited a great Christian tradition in this country and there is in fact a good deal of religion about and plenty of churches to look into and occasions in which to join. Life is an island with three corners, of birth, marriage and death, and from these points people look out to sea; though they may be hazy, here is some very real reaching out to faith. But many retreat into repeating familiar phrases, but keeping God at arm's length. There is much good in the familiar phrases, but at arm's length we lose the thought of his help and grace, and become complacent in the process; this was a danger to both Puritans and Victorians. It is a danger for those who rest in the Book of Common Prayer and its splendid Elizabethan language and do not examine its roots in the theology of the judgment and grace of God. There is the further point that the wordiness of the language of Cranmer makes us overlook how much his theology misses out about creation, about resurrection, and about the transformation of society. The vigour of Cranmer's writing came from the fact that he himself was a reformer and saw the need to bring the gospel of Christ to bear on the transformation of the Church. He was not in a position to see the further need for transformation of both society and theology. He was, however, one who saw that the Church needed constantly to be reformed; in his own preface in the Prayer Book he gives the clue to the need of an alternative book today 'in such a Language and Order as is most easy and plain for the understanding both of the Readers and Hearers'.

That quotation may remind us of a passage in the epistle of James, 'Be sure that you act on the message and do not merely listen, for that would be to mislead yourselves'. This applies both within worship as well as to the results of worship. A great danger of conventional worship is that it becomes one of listening, and maybe singing, only. There is no lifting up or reaching out to receive God's judgment in grace. We must go on from hearing the gospel to 'do this' as Jesus said, and receive him in the sacrament, so that we may go out to share that dying and rising life in the world. Listening and singing very easily stop at the church door, and conform to conventional views about the world, which protect our own advantages.

There is a much better use for the great stretches of post-Christian survivals we find in society. There is much with words and music that can be done with people's belief to help them to realise that they want more. They can be enabled to discover the generosity of God in his self-giving and trust; 'O Lamb of God' has a long and wide appeal. 'O taste and see' is an invitation to all. The old phrases blend with great music from the past; they need to be used meditatively, with time to ponder the deep meanings of the meeting with Christ. Those words and music need to be used thoughtfully: they need, in fact, the clear structure and words of the revised orders to make them meaningful. The rubrics of the revised services enable the old words to be used for settings written for them within the structure of the revised service. The period after communion, when the vessels are cleansed, is a particularly suitable time for traditional phrases and music in canticles and motets: these become more vivid as people grow in a worship which comes to have real meaning for them.

*   *   *   *   *

There is mystery enough for Christian men and women to explore today; the revised liturgies and alternative services put into our hands the means to make exploration. We discover that we are invited into a transcendent and transforming intimacy with God in Christ –

'We remember his offering of himself
made once for all upon the cross
and proclaim his mighty resurrection and glorious ascension.
As we look for his coming in glory,
we celebrate with this bread and this cup
his one perfect sacrifice.
Accept through him, our great high priest,
this our sacrifice of thanks and praise;
and as we eat and drink these holy gifts
in the presence of your divine majesty,
renew us by your Spirit,
inspire us with your love,
and unite us in the body of your Son,
Jesus Christ our Lord.'

This is a wonderful invitation to accept. It is a call from our Father who does not keep us at arm's length, but calls us to take his help and come near. It is a call to all who drop in occasionally to become his regular friends and companions, not for cosiness, but for renewal and inspiration to share in his transforming work in the world. His life is to be taken out into home, into work, and into society. Obviously it is a life to be held in common with all Christians, but even more so it is a life to be shared with those who do not at present share faith. All this has to be worked out in a world which in parts is oblivious, and in others rather forgetful; it is a world which owes its life and its responsibility to its creator and redeemer, yet where men and women forget that they owe care and responsibility one to another. This life shared with Christ has to be worked out in active love which is prepared to recreate relationship within society at every level. There is a vast amount of work to be done here. We have to learn to use positively the half belief of many of our fellows, the residue of a post-Christian society, but not be held back by its conventional bands.

Christianity is too important to be treated in this way. It is not just a comfort for tired men and women, or a hobby to be enjoyed on the side; it is about the reconciliation of the world, the reconciliation of men and women with their creator, made possible in Christ. In the division of our society, and amid the rootlessness, and search for identity of many within it, there is urgent need to help men and women discover the reconciliation offered to us in Christ. It is not a distant and theoretical belief which Christianity has to offer; it is the good news of God meeting us in Christ, much more simply than people often realise. He is willing to put into our hands the simple focus of faith, which Christ gave his disciples as he went to his death, and which was made available for them by his resurrection. 'Do this', Jesus said, 'Take, eat and drink'. We need to find communion with him and help others to do so, and so with each other, to share in the renewal and reconciliation of his whole world. As we do this and 'shew the Lord's death till he come', we can echo the words of the prayer from the Alternative Service Book –

Eternal God,
you have declared in Christ
the completion of your purpose of love.
May we live by faith, walk in hope,
and be renewed in love,
until the world reflects your glory,
and you are all in all.
Even so; come, Lord Jesus.